Idaho State Department

General School Laws of the State of Idaho

Idaho State Department

General School Laws of the State of Idaho

ISBN/EAN: 9783744667005

Printed in Europe, USA, Canada, Australia, Japan

Cover: Foto ©Suzi / pixelio.de

More available books at **www.hansebooks.com**

General School Laws

OF THE

STATE OF IDAHO.

Compiled by

PERMEAL FRENCH,

Superintendent of Public Instruction State of Idaho.

1899-1900

DEMOCRATIC-TIMES' JOB ROOM,
Moscow, Idaho.
1899.

GENERAL INFORMATION.

Certificates.

Life Diplomas, State Certificates, and County Certificates are granted *only on examination.*

Applicants for Life Diplomas are examined in the following: Political Economy, Zoology, Psychology, Plane Geometry.

Applicants for State Certificates are examined in the following: Physics, Literature, General History, Botany, Paper.

Applicants for County Certificates are examined in the following: Arithmetic, Grammar, United States History, Civil Government, Geography, State Constitution, Physiology, Reading. School-Law, Theory and Art. Algebra.

Application for Life Diploma and State Certificate is not considered unless applicant holds a first-grade County Certificate. issued by a County Superintendent of this State.

Laws Relating to Common Schools.

CHAPTER I.—State Board of Public Instruction.

Section 1.—*Members and Officers.* The Superintendent of Public Instruction, the Secretary of State, and the Attorney General shall constitute the State Board of Public Instruction, of which the Superintendent shall be President. The Board shall have power to appoint a Secretary.

Sec. 2.—*Regular Meetings.* The Board of Public Instruction shall meet at the Capitol on the first Monday of June and December of each year for the transaction of business and at such other times as its President shall direct; and shall have power to adopt rules and regulations, not inconsistent with the laws of this State, for its own government.

Sec. 3.—*State Examinations—Assistants—Compensation.* The State Board shall hold annually, at least two public examinations of teachers, at each of which examinations one member of the Board shall preside, assisted by such person, or persons, not to exceed two in number, as the Board may select, who shall receive for such services not to exceed five dollars per day, and said Board shall keep a full and correct record of its proceedings and a complete register of all persons to whom certificates are issued.

Sec. 4—*State Certificates and State Diplomas—When Granted.* Said Board shall issue State Certificates and State Diplomas to those persons only, who possess good moral character and who shall have passed a thorough examination in all the branches included in the Course of Study prescribed for the public schools of the State, didactics and such other branches as the Board may direct. *Provided,* That in no case shall a State Certificate be granted unless the applicant has been successfully engaged in teaching for at least three years and can furnish the Board satisfactory evidence of his or her ability to instruct and properly manage any school in the State. Such certificate shall authorize the person to whom it is issued to teach in any public school in the State for the term of five years from the date of its issue, unless sooner revoked by the State Board of Public Instruction.

Sec. 5.—*State Diploma—Conditions.* In no case shall a State Diploma be granted, unless the applicant has been successfully engaged in teaching for the term of at least five years, two of which shall have been in the State of Idaho, and can furnish the Board satisfactory evidence of his ability to instruct and properly manage any public school in the State. Such diploma shall authorize the person to whom it is issued to teach in any public school of the State during the life-time of the holder, unless revoked by the State Board of Public Instruction.

SEC. 6.—*Recognition of Other State Diplomas.* The Board may issue certificates to persons holding State Diplomas or State Certificates from other States requiring similar qualifications.

SEC. 7.—*Revocation of Certificates.* The State Board of Public Instruction shall have the power to revoke any State Certificate or State Diploma, for any cause or disqualification, which would have been sufficient ground for refusing to issue the same, had the cause existed or been known at the time of its issue. *Provided.* That before revoking any such certificate or diploma the holder thereof shall have at least thirty days' notice to appear before the State Board and show cause why such revocation should not be made.

CHAPTER II.—STATE SUPERINTENDENT OF PUBLIC INSTRUCTION.

SECTION 1.—*Official Qualification.* Before entering upon the duties of his office the State Superintendent of Public Instruction shall take and subscribe to the oath, prescribed by the Constitution, and execute a bond in the penal sum of two thousand dollars, payable to the State of Idaho, with sureties to be approved by the Governor, conditioned upon the faithful performance of his official duties, and the delivery to his successor of all books, papers, documents and other property belonging to the office. Said bond and oath shall be deposited with the Secretary of State.

SEC. 2.—*Office at Seat of Government—Preservation of Records.* He shall have an office at the Capitol, where a seal shall be kept which shall be the official seal of the State Superintendent of Public Instruction, by which all his official acts may be authenticated, and all records, books, and papers appertaining to the business of this office. He shall file all papers, reports, and public documents transmitted to him by the County Superintendents of the several counties and hold the same in readiness to be exhibited to the Governor, or to any Committee of any House of the Legislature, or any citizen of the State.

SEC. 3.—*Supervision of Schools—Course of Study.* He shall have general supervision of all the County Superintendents and of the public schools of the State, and shall prepare and prescribe a Course of Study for use in all such public schools.

SEC. 4.—*Teachers' Examination.* He shall prepare or cause to be prepared all examination questions to be used by the County Superintendents of the several counties of the State in the examination of applicants for teachers' certificates, and shall prescribe the rules and regulations for the conducting of all such examinations.

SEC. 5.—*Conference with County Superintendents.* He shall meet the County Superintendents of each judicial district, or of two or more districts combined, at such time and place as he shall appoint, giving them due notice of such meeting. The object of such meeting shall be to accumulate facts relative to schools, to compare views, to discuss principles, to hear discussions and suggestions appertaining to the examination and qualification of teachers, methods of instruction, institutes and all other matters embraced in the public school system.

SEC. 6.—*School Laws.* He shall have the law relating to the public schools printed in pamphlet form and shall supply school officers, school libraries and State Librarians with one copy each of such pamphlets; said printing to be paid for on the warrant of the Auditor out of the General Fund on bills approved by the State Board of Examiners.

SEC. 7.—*Biennial Report.* He shall on or before the first day of December in every year preceding that in which shall be held a regular session of the Legislature, report to the Governor the condition of the public schools, the amount of State School Fund apportioned and sources from which derived, with such suggestions and recommendations relating to the affairs of his office as he may think proper.

SEC. 8.—*Visitation of Schools.* It shall be his duty to visit annually such counties of the State as most need his personal attendance, and all counties if practicable, for the purpose of inspecting the schools, awakening and guiding public sentiment in relation to the practical interests of education. And he shall open such correspondence as may enable him to obtain all necessary information relating to the system of public schools in other states.

SEC. 9.—*Traveling Expenses and Incidentals.* He shall receive out of the State Treasury for actual traveling expenses and other expenses while traveling on the business of the department, not exceeding seven hundred and fifty dollars per annum, for which he shall render an itemized bill to the State Board of Examiners; and all office fuel, furniture, books, postage, stationery and other contingent expenses pertaining to his office, shall be furnished in the same manner as those of the other departments of the State government.

SEC. 10.—*Apportionment of School Funds.* The income of the State School Fund and taxes collected by the State for the support of the public schools which will be received up to the first day of January and the first day of July of each year shall be distributed semi-annually during said months respectively in each year among the several counties of the State from which reports have been received by the State Superintendent of Public Instruction, as provided in this act, in proportion to the number of children of school age, as shown by the last school census list of each county, and the Superintendent of Public Instruction shall certify such apportionment to the State Auditor, and upon such certificate the Auditor shall draw his warrant in favor of the County Treasurer of each county, for the amount due such county. The Superintendent shall also certify to the Treasurer and Superintendent of each county the amount apportioned to each county.

CHAPTER III.—County Superintendents.

An Act to Establish the Office of County Superintendent of Public Instruction and Prescribing the Duties of the Same.

Be it enacted by the Legislature of the State of Idaho:

SEC. 1.—*Election of County Superintendents.* At the next ensuing general election after the passage of this act, there shall be elected in each county in the State of Idaho, a Superintendent of Public Instruction, who shall reside at the county seat of the county in which he is elected, and who shall hold his office for a term of two years, from and after his taking charge of the same and until his successor has been elected and qualified.

SEC. 2.—*Official Qualifications.* Before entering upon the duties of his office the County Superintendent of Public Instruction shall take and subscribe the oath prescribed by law and execute a bond, payable to the State of Idaho, with two or more sureties to be approved by the Board of County Commissioners, in the penal sum of not less than two thousand dollars, conditioned upon the faithful performance of his official duties, and the delivery of all moneys and property received by him as such Superintendent to his successor in office, which bond shall be filed in the office of the County Recorder; which official bond, together with his official oath, shall be filed in the office of the County Recorder as aforesaid, not later than the second Monday in January, next after election. *Provided,* That no person shall be eligible to the office of County Superintendent of Public Instruction except a practical teacher of not less than two years' experience and the holder of a valid First Grade Certificate, at the time of his election or appointment.

SEC. 3.—*Supervision and Visitation.* The County Superintendent of Public Instruction shall have charge and oversight of the public schools of his county, and it shall be his duty to visit every public school in his county at least once during each term and remain at said public school at least one-half day. At such visits he shall carefully observe the methods employed by the teacher in giving instruction in the several branches taught; the manner of discipline and government, the classification of the pupils, and the general management of the schools, and shall give the schools such instruction and encouragement as he deems for the best interest of all concerned, and he shall make such suggestions to the teacher in private as, in his judgment, will render the said teacher more efficient, and promote the general educational interests of the districts.

SEC. 4.—*Office at the County Seat—Distribution of Blanks.* The County Commissioners shall furnish the County Superintendent of Public Instruction an office at the county seat, and they shall furnish him with all necessary office furniture, including seal and blank books, stationery, postage, expressage, all blanks necessary for his office, and all blank books and blanks necessary for the use of the Trustees and teachers in the discharge of their respective official duties in his county. The County

Superintendent of Public Instruction shall designate certain days in each month as his office days, which shall not be less than five in any month, and upon these days so designated by him, he shall keep his office open from 9 o'clock A. M. until o'clock 5 P. M.

SEC. 5.—*Direction to Trustees.* He may, in his discretion, require the Trustees in any district to repair the school buildings or property, or to abate any nuisance in and about the premises, if such repair or abatement can be done for a sum not to exceed seventy-five dollars. *Provided,* There is a sufficient amount of money in the treasury to the credit of the district. He may also, in all cases, require the Trustees to provide suitable outhouses; and in case the Trustees fail to make such provision within a reasonable time, he may cause it to be done and draw an order for a warrant, as hereinafter provided, upon the County Auditor for said expenses, who shall draw his warrant payable out of any money to the credit of such district.

SEC. 6.—*Record of Official Acts.* He shall keep a complete record of all his official acts; preserve all blanks, maps, charts and apparatus, sent him as such officer, and file all papers, reports and statements from teachers and school boards; keep a record of all teachers employed in his county, giving name of teacher, number of district, salary per month, grade of certificate and date of Superintendent's visit. He shall obey the legal instructions of the State Superintendent.

SEC. 7.—*Examinations—Regular—Special—Official Notice.* He shall hold one regular public examination in each year for the purpose of examining all persons who may offer themselves as teachers in the public schools; said examination to be held in some suitable room at the county seat, and commencing on the fourth Thursday of August and continuing not to exceed three days. And for a like purpose the said County Superintendent shall hold not to exceed three special examinations at such times and places as in his judgment the interests of the schools and teachers of the county shall require. *Provided,* That it shall be the duty of the County Superintendent to give at least fifteen days' notice of such regular and special public examinations in some newspaper published in the county.

SEC. 8.—*Teachers' Certificates—Qualifications—Signatures* He shall grant certificates to teachers in such form as the State Superintendent of Public Instruction shall prescribe, and to those persons only who shall have attained the age of eighteen years, who have attended the said public examination and shall be found to possess good moral character, thorough scholarship, and the ability to instruct and govern a school; but no certificate shall be granted to any person who shall not pass a satisfactory examination in Orthography, Reading, Writing, Grammar, Arithmetic, Geography, History of the United States, Civil Government, Physiology and Hygiene, with particular reference to the effects of Alcoholic Drinks, Stimulants and Narcotics upon the Human System, Theory and Practice of Teaching, State Constitution, and so much of the General School Laws as relates to the duties and responsibilities of teaching. All certificates shall be signed by the County Superintendent. and no person shall be considered a qualified teacher within the meaning of the School Law, who has not a certificate granted by the said Superintendent or other lawful authority. *Provided,* That all examination questions shall have been prepared as prescribed by law, furnished under seal and opened before the applicants for certificates on the day of examination. *Provided,* That First Grade Certificates shall be granted to all applicants who are otherwise qualified according to law, and who shall have passed all the branches required in this section, and Algebra in addition thereto, with a general average of not less than ninety per cent., and with a minimum of not less than seventy-five per cent. in any branch, and all applicants who are otherwise qualified according to law, shall be granted Second Grade Certificates who shall have attained a general average of eighty per cent., and a minimum in any branch of not less than seventy per cent., and Third Grade Certificates shall be granted to all applicants who are otherwise qualified according to law, who shall have attained a general average of seventy-five per cent., and a minimum in any branch of not less than sixty per cent. *Provided, further,* That each applicant for teacher's certificate under the provisions of this act shall pay the County Superintendent the sum of one dollar, the same to be deposited by him in the county treasury to the credit of the Institute Fund, to be used in institute work in addition to the regular appropriation.

SEC. 9.—*Teachers' Certificates—Grades.* The certificates issued by the County Superintendent, subject to the rules and regulations prescribed by the State Superintendent, shall be of three grades: (1.) First grades, which shall be valid in the county in which they are issued for a term of three years from the date thereof unless sooner revoked, and they shall be good in any county in the State for the same period by the holder thereof filing a certified copy of the same with the County Superintendent in the county in which he desires to teach. (2.) Second Grade Certificates, which shall entitle the holder to teach in the county in and for which they are issued, for a term of two years. (3.) Third grades, which shall be valid in the county where issued for a term of one year.

SEC. 10.—*Revocation of Certificates.* The County Superintendent of Public Instruction shall have power to revoke any teacher's certificate, other than those granted by the State Superintendent, for neglect of duty, for incompetency to instruct and govern a school, for immorality or for any cause or disqualification which would have been sufficient ground for refusing to issue the same had the cause existed or been known at the time of its issue. *Provided,* That no certificate shall be revoked or annulled without a personal hearing, unless the holder thereof shall, after reasonable notice, neglect or refuse to appear before the Superintendent for that purpose.

SEC. 11. —*Record of Certificates.* He shall keep a record of all certificates granted or revoked, showing to whom issued, age of grantee, date of issue, grade and duration of each certificate, and if revoked, date and reason therefor.

SEC. 12. —*Annual Report.* He shall, on or before the first day of October in each year, make and transmit an Annual Report to the State Superintendent for the school year ending August 31st, next preceding, which report shall contain an abstract of all reports made to him by the District Clerks of the several districts of the county, together with such statistics, items and statements, relative to the schools of the county, as may be required and prescribed by the State Superintendent. Such reports shall be made upon and conform to the blanks furnished by the State Superintendent for that purpose. He shall inquire and ascertain whether the boundaries of the school districts in his county are definitely and plainly described in the records of the Clerk of the Board of County Commissioners, and to keep in his office a full and correct transcript of such boundaries. In case the boundaries of districts are conflicting or incorrectly described, he shall report such fact to the Board of County Commissioners at their regular meeting in July, and such Board shall immediately take such steps as are necessary to change, harmonize and clearly define them. The County Superintendent, if he deems it necessary for the guidance of School Census Marshals, may order the description of the district boundaries printed in pamphlet form, to be paid out of the Current Expense Fund of the county.

SEC. 13.—*Appointments—New Districts—Vacancies.* The County Superintendent shall appoint Trustees for all newly organized school districts who shall serve until the next regular election, fill all vacancies that may occur in the Board of Trustees by reason of death, resignation or otherwise, and such appointments shall hold until the next regular election.

SEC. 14.—*Necessary Expenses.* The County Superintendent shall be allowed all necessary expenses incurred in the examination of teachers, for blanks, books, stationery, pens and inks, out of the Current Expense Fund of the county.

SEC. 15.—*Apportionment of School Funds.* The County Superintendent shall require of the County Treasurer quarterly each year, a report of the amount of money on hand to the credit of the School Fund of each county, not already apportioned, and the County Treasurer shall furnish such report when so required. The County Superintendent upon receiving such report shall proceed to apportion the public school moneys, both county and State, reported by the County Treasurer, to be in the county treasury, among the several school districts in the following manner, to-wit: One-third of the whole amount he shall divide equally among the several districts that have complied with the provisions of this act. The remaining two-thirds of said whole amount he shall apportion per capita among the several districts in proportion to the number of children in each district as shown by the last report of the Census Marshal of each district, and credit each district with the amount to which the apportionment entitles. *Provided*, That each district is entitled to one share in the apportionment of the first one-third, regardless of the number of children therein. Immediately after such apportionment he shall certify to the County Treasurer the amounts which are to be placed to the credit of each district and notify the Clerk of each district of the amount placed to the credit of his district.

SEC. 16.—*Neglect of Duty—Penalty*. If the County Superintendent fails to make a full and correct report to the State Superintendent of Public Instruction of all statements required by law to be made, he forfeits the sum of one hundred dollars from any moneys due him from the county, and the Board of County Commissioners are hereby authorized and required to deduct therefrom the sum aforesaid upon information from the State Superintendent of Public Instruction, that such reports have not been made.

SEC. 17.—*To Whom Issue Certificates*. No certificate shall be granted or teacher employed in any of the public schools of this State to any person not a citizen of the United States.

SEC. 18.—*Repealing Clause*. All acts and parts of acts in conflict with this act are hereby repealed.

SEC. 19.—*Salary County Superintendent*. The County Superintendent of Public Instruction shall receive a salary of not less than five hundred dollars ($500) per annum, and not to exceed fifteen hundred dollars ($1500) per annum.

CHAPTER IV.—DISTRICT TRUSTEES.

SEC. 1.—*Board—How Composed*. At the next regular school election, following the passage of this act, there must be elected a Board of Trustees consisting of three in number, one of whom must hold office for three years, one for two years and one for one year, and the ballots must designate the length of time which said Trustees are to serve. At the second and every subsequent school election there must be elected one Trustee for the term of three years.

SEC. 2.—*Organization*. Immediately after their election they must elect from their number a Chairman and Clerk.

SEC. 3.—*Regular Meetings*. The regular meeting of the Board of Trustees shall be held on the last Saturday of March, June, September and December. The Board may, however, hold other special or adjourned meetings, as they may from time to time determine.

SEC. 4.—*Quorum*. Any two of said Trustees shall constitute a quorum for the transaction of business.

SEC. 5.—*Employment and Dismissal of Teachers—Compensation of Clerk and Tuition of Pupils*. It shall be the duty of the Trustees of each district to employ teachers, on a written contract, and to discharge the same, and to fix, allow and order paid their salaries and compensation, and the compensation of the Clerk of the Board, and to determine the rate of tuition of non-resident pupils, and they shall have power to discharge any teacher for any neglect of duty, or any cause that in their opinion, renders the service of such teacher unprofitable to the district, but no teacher shall be discharged before the end of his term without a reasonable hearing.

SEC. 6.—*Charge of School Property.* The Trustees shall have charge of all school property in their district, and have power to receive in trust all real estate or other property conveyed to said school district, and to convey by deed, duly executed or delivered, all the estate or interest of their district in any school house or site directed to be sold by a vote of their district; and all conveyance made to said Board must be made in their corporate name: To the Trustees of School District No......, County ...., State of Idaho.

SEC. 7.—*Power to Purchase Real Estate, Etc.* Said Trustees have further power when directed by a vote of their district, to purchase, receive, hold and convey real and personal property for school purposes, and to hold, purchase and repair school houses and to supply the same with necessary furniture and to fix the location of school houses.

SEC. 8.—*Pecuniary Interest.* No Trustee shall be pecuniarily interested in any contract made by the Board of Trustees of which he is a member, and any contract made in violation of this section is null and void.

SEC. 9.—*Furnish Necessary Supplies—Limit of Such Purchase.* The Trustees of the respective districts must furnish all things, not herein otherwise provided for, necessary for the use and comfort of the schools in their district, such as fuel, improvements, maps, apparatus, a library, and for such purpose may audit and allow accounts against the School Fund of their district, not to exceed twenty-five per cent. of the amount of such School Fund in any one year.

SEC. 10.—*Orders for Warrants.* That the Trustees shall not draw an order for a warrant in excess of the amount to the credit of the district at the time the order is given.

SEC. 11.—*Annual Report.* The Trustees of each district must make a full report in writing, annually, on the 1st day of September, to the County Superintendent of their county, on blanks furnished, relating to all matters pertaining to schools as may be required of them by the State or County Superintendent.

SEC. 12.—*Suspension of Pupils.* It is the duty of the Trustees of the respective districts on receiving a report from any teacher of the disorderly conduct of any pupil, to decide how said insubordinate pupil shall be punished, or whether he or she be dismissed from school, and the teacher must enforce the decision so made.

SEC. 13.—*Enumeration of Children.* The Clerk of the Board of Trustees must, on the first Monday of July of each year, proceed to enumerate the children of school age in his district, and he must not enumerate any except bona fide residents thereof, and the Board of Trustees must cause a true and certified copy of said census to be transmitted to the County Superintendent.

SEC. 14.—*Compensation for Enumeration.* For said service said Clerk shall be allowed as full compensation therefor five cents for each child so enumerated, and the Chairman of the Board of Trustees shall draw his order upon the County Auditor, which must be countersigned by at least one other member of the Board of said district for the amount so allowed, and it must be charged against and paid out of the fund of said county [district.]

SEC. 15.—*Non Resident Pupils.* Trustees may determine whether pupils outside of their district may attend school in such district, and upon what terms. (Laws 1893, Ch. 5, Sec. 35.) When it shall appear that a pupil living in one district cannot attend school in his or her own district because of the distance of the school house and for other reasons, then when convenient, by an agreement of the Trustees of the respective districts, he or she may attend a school in an adjoining district and that district shall receive for said pupil's tuition from the said pupil's district, such an amount as said pupil would be credited with in said pupil's own district.

CHAPTER V.—SCHOOL DISTRICTS.

SECTION 1.—*Corporation—How Constituted.* Each regularly organized school district in this State is hereby declared to be a body corporate by the name and style of School District Number ......, in the County of............, State of Idaho; and in that name the Trustees may sue and be sued, hold and convey property for the use and benefit of such district and make contracts the same as municipal corporations in this State.

SEC. 2.—*New Districts and Change of Boundaries—When Done.* The Board of County Commissioners of several counties of the State shall have power to create new districts from unorganized territory or from old districts, to change the boundaries of any district heretofore established or to attach to one or more school districts the territory included within the boundaries of any district which shall lapse by reason of the failure to comply with the provisions of this act: *Provided,* That no district shall be formed from any territory, or the boundaries of any district be changed at any other time than at the regular quarterly meetings of the board, nor at that time unless a petition for such new district or the change of boundaries is filed in the office of County Superintendent on or before the fifteenth day of the month preceding.

SEC. 3.—*Petition—Contents Of.* If such petition is for a new district it must set forth the boundaries of the new district asked for and must be signed by the parents or guardians of at least ten children of school age who are residents of the proposed new district ; and if for a change of boundaries, such petition must set forth the change of boundaries desired and the reasons for the same, and must be signed by at least two-thirds of those who are heads of families and residents of the territory embraced within the limits of the tract to be stricken off or added to a district.

SEC. 4.—*Petition—Notice to Parties—Presentation to Commissioners.* It shall be the duty of the County Superintendent upon receipt of any petition, as herein provided for, to immediately give notice to all parties interested by sending notice by registered mail to each of the Trustees of the district to be affected by such change or changes; and cause printed notices to be posted in at least three public places in the districts so affected, one of which shall be on the door of the school house in said district, for at least one week. Such notice must state the change or changes to be made in said district, that the petition is on file in the office of the County Superintendent, and that the same will be presented to the Board of County Commissioners at their regular meeting for their final action. The Superintendent must transmit the said petition to the said Board with his approval or disapproval, and if he approve the same he may note such changes in boundaries as in his judgment shall be for the best interest of all parties concerned.

SEC. 5.—*Petition—County Commissioners Must Act.* The Board of County Commissioners must, at their next regular meeting, act upon the same. If such petition be granted it may be in accordance with the original prayer, or with such modifications as they may choose to make.

SEC. 6—*Union of Districts—Division—When Allowed—Area.* Two or more districts lying contiguous may, upon a petition of the majority of the heads of families residing in each of said districts, be united to constitute one district: *Provided, also,* That no district shall be hereafter divided for the purpose of forming a new district unless it contains an area of more than nine square miles ; nor shall a new district be divided, if by so doing the remainder of the district shall be found to contain less than fifteen persons of school age, nor shall any incorporated city or town, hereafter be divided into two or more districts.

SEC. 7.—*Joint Districts—How Formed.* A joint school district may be formed from territory belonging to two or more contiguous counties. For the purpose of organizing a joint district the same preliminary steps must be taken, and the same course be pursued, as is pursued in the organization of other districts, as is provided in Sec. 35* and 36* of this act. Such districts shall be designated as "Joint District No...., of the counties of......" and be so numbered that it shall have the same number in all the counties from which it was formed. The petition required by Sec. 35* shall be made to each County Superintendent interested.

SEC. 8—*Record of Joint Districts.* The school census, the record of attendance at school, the assessing of property, the col-

*Section 6. Chapter 5.   *Section 4. Chapter 5.

section of taxes, and all acts which from their nature shall be separately kept, shall be kept and done, and the report thereof made as if each portion of said joint district were an entire district in the respective counties. The teacher of such joint district shall not be required to hold a certificate in both counties.

SEC. 9.—*New Districts—Entitled to Apportionment.* All new districts formed of unorganized territory shall be entitled to their just proportion of school moneys at the next apportionment and the County Superintendent shall place the same to the credit of such district: *Provided,* That in no case shall such district be entitled to use the same unless school has actually been commenced therein and six months shall not have elapsed since the date of its organization.

SEC. 10.—*New Districts—Adjustment of Funds or Indebtedness.* If any new district is organized from any part of any other organized district or districts, as provided in this act, the County Superintendent, after having ascertained the amount of moneys belonging to said old district or districts and deducting said indebtedness and liabilities, must apportion to said new district its due per capita proportion of money or indebtedness, as the case may be, from said districts from which it may be formed.

SEC. 11.—*Joint Districts—Apportionment.* [Laws 1893, Ch. 5, Sec. 39.] And in case of joint districts the County Superintendent must apportion to such district such proportion of the school money to which such district is entitled, as the number of school children residing in that portion of the district situated in his county bears to the whole number of school census children in the whole district.

SEC. 12.—*Dissolution of Districts—When—Sale of Property —Disposal of Territory.* If any school district shall, for the period of one year, fail to maintain a school for a term of at least three consecutive months or keep up its organization of officers, as required by law, or if there has been an average attendance for three consecutive months of only five pupils, or less, such district shall lapse, and the moneys in the treasury of the county belonging thereto shall be apportioned by the County Superintendent among the other districts in the same manner as other school moneys are apportioned. The property of any school district that shall lapse shall be sold by the County Superintendent in such manner as he shall deem best. The proceeds of such sale, after the payment of any indebtedness of said district, shall be placed to the credit of the General School Fund. The territory included within the boundaries of the said district shall, by order of the Board of County Commissioners, be attached to one or more school districts.

CHAPTER VI.—SCHOOL ELECTIONS—SPECIAL TAX.

SEC. 1. The regular election for electing members of the Board of School Trustees shall be held annually in each district on the first Monday in June at which time it shall be lawful to transact any business pertaining to schools and school interests. The Clerk of said Board of Trustees shall cause printed or written notices to be posted specifying the time and place of holding such election and the time during which the ballot box shall be kept open, not less, however, than three hours, and further specifying at what hour other business shall be transacted. Said notice shall be posted in three public places in the district, one of which shall be the school house, if there be one, at least ten days previous to such time of election. If the Clerk fail to give such notice, then any two legal voters residing in the district may give such notice over their own names, and such election may be held after the day fixed in this Act for such election. All elections shall be by ballot; the polls shall be opened by one of the Board of Trustees, or by any qualified elector if no Trustee be present at the time specified in the notice. If no time is specified in the notice, then the polls shall be opened at one o'clock P. M. and closed at five P. M. of the same day. Said election shall be conducted as any other county election, except that one Judge and one Clerk may constitute a Board of Election, and any Trustee may administer the oath to the said Judge and Clerk. Said Judge and Clerk shall make return of such election to the County Superintendent immediately, which return shall be filed in the office of the County Superintendent: *Provided, further,* That it shall be lawful at such annual meeting and election on said first Monday in June to vote upon the question of whether or not any special tax shall be levied for any purpose, such as building or repairing school houses, or for the support of public schools in the district; said meeting may first decide the rate to be levied, not to exceed ten mills on the dollar of taxable property, then proceed to ballot, on which ballot shall be written or printed "Tax—Yes" or "Tax--No" and none but actual resident freeholders or heads of families of said district are entitled to vote at such election: *Provided,* That for the purpose of this Act both husband and wife are to be considered a head of a family. A separate ballot box shall be used for voting on any question of taxation or other business concerning schools and school interests, from that used in voting for Trustees. If a majority of the votes polled at such election are in favor of a tax, the Board of Trustees must immediately make such levy and certify the fact, the date thereof, and the rate of tax levied, the year for which levied and the number of the district, to the Clerk of the Board of County Commissioners and the County Assessors, but not more than one such special tax shall be levied in any one year.

SEC. 2. — *Qualified Voters — General School Election.* (Const. Art. 6, Sec. 2.) Except as in this article otherwise provided, every male citizen of the United States, twenty-one years old, who has actually resided in the state or territory for six months, and in the county where he offers to vote, thirty days next preceding the day of election, is a qualified elector; and until otherwise provided by the legislature, women who have the qualifications prescribed in this article, may continue to hold such school offices and vote at such school elections as provided by the laws of Idaho.

SEC. 3.— *When and How Trustees Qualify.* Trustees must qualify within fifteen days after receiving notice of their election, by taking the official oath, which oath may be administered by either of the other Trustees or the retiring Trustee, and said oath shall be subscribed and filed in the office of the County Superintendent.

CHAPTER VII.—SCHOOL FUNDS.

SEC. 1.— *Proceeds of Lands.* The Public School Fund of the State shall consist of the proceeds of such lands as have heretofore been granted, or may hereafter be granted, to the State by the general government known as "School Lands" and those granted in lieu of such. Lands acquired by gift or grant from any person or corporation under any law or grant, and of all other grants of land or money made to the State for general educational purposes, and all moneys accruing to the State from the estates of deceased persons.

SEC. 2.— *Funds Shall Remain Inviolate and Intact* (Const. Ch. 9, Sec. 3.) The Public School Fund of the State shall forever remain inviolate and intact; the interest thereon only shall be expended in the maintenance of the schools of the State, and shall be distributed among the several counties and school districts of the State in such manner as may be prescribed by law. No part of this fund, principal or interest, shall ever be transferred to any other fund, or used or appropriated except as herein provided. The State Treasurer shall be the custodian of this fund, and the same shall be securely and profitably invested as may be by law directed. The State shall supply all losses thereof that may in any manner occur.

SEC. 3.— *School Tax Levy.* For the purpose of establishing and maintaining public schools in the several counties of the State, the Board of County Commissioners shall, at the time of levying the taxes for the State and county purposes, levy a tax of not less than five mills nor more than ten mills on each dollar of taxable property, in their respective counties, for school purposes. Said taxes must be assessed and collected in each county as other taxes for State and county purposes.

FREE SCHOOL SYSTEM—AMENDING OF.
An Act to Amend Sections Thirty-one and Thirty-three of an Act Entitled, "An Act to Establish and Maintain a System of Free Schools."

SEC. 4.— *Free School System — Amending Of — Duty of County Treasurer—District not Entitled to Apportionment— Duty of County Auditor—Repeal—Approval.* That Section 31 of said act be amended to read as follows: Sec. 31. It is hereby made the duty of the County Treasurer to keep a separate account with each school district in the county ; to place to the credit of each, the amount of money certified to by the County Superintendent, as provided in this act, and to pay over the money on legally drawn warrants or orders of the district officers entitled to draw the same: *Provided.* That if the County Superintendent shall notify the County Treasurer in writing, that there has been a failure on the part of any Board of Trustees to comply with the law, and that said money shall be withheld from said Board of Trustees, he shall retain the same until further notice from the County Superintendent. All moneys that shall be finally forfeited by any district shall be put into the General School Fund of the county, and be apportioned as other moneys. And it shall be the duty of said Treasurer to receive and hold as special deposits all moneys belonging to the Public School Fund of his county in accordance with the provisions of this act, and to pay them over only on the warrant of the County Auditor: *Provided, further,* That the said County Treasurer shall pay over to the Treasurer of any independent school district organized under the provisions of this act, all moneys belonging to such district upon the presentation of an order from the Clerk of the Board of Trustees of such district signed also by the Chairman thereof, and countersigned by the County Superintendent and County Auditor. (Special Act 1897, H. B. 73, Sec. 2.) That Sec. 33 of said act be amended to read as follows: Sec. 33. It shall be the duty of the County Auditor upon the presentation of any order from the Clerk of the Board of Trustees of any school district in his county, said order also being signed by the Chairman of the said Board of Trustees or in his absence by the other member of the Board, to draw his warrant upon the School Fund standing to the credit of said district in favor of the person mentioned in the said order: *Provided.* That in case of independent school district orders, he shall not draw his warrant, but countersign the warrant or order of said district officers: *Provided further,* That the said orders have been countersigned by the County Superintendent, but in no case shall he issue a warrant, or countersign an order for a greater amount than there is cash in the treasury to the credit of said district.

Sec. 3. All acts and parts of acts in conflict with this act are hereby repealed.

Sec. 5. *Duty of County Superintendent.* It shall be the duty of the County Superintendent in each county to keep a separate account with each school district in his county; to place to the credit of each district the amount apportioned by him as provided for in this act; to countersign all legally drawn warrants and orders of the district officers entitled to draw the same; to enter the same upon his books in proper form, giving date, number of such warrant, or order, to whom drawn, for what purpose, and the amount of the same.

Sec. 6.—*Collection of Penal Fines.* It shall be the duty of the County Superintendent to collect by process of law all penal fines not paid over by the Justices of the Peace, or other officers required by law to pay the same into the county treasury; and the same may be collected and recovered by action at law, in which the State of Idaho, by the County Superintendent, is plaintiff and the officer neglecting or refusing to pay over said moneys is defendant.

SEC. 7.—*Special Tax Levy—Duty of Assessor.* Upon receiving such statement from the Trustees of any school district the Assessor must assess upon all property in the district subject to taxation the tax so levied and certified to him as aforesaid; but for that purpose he is not required to take new statements from the owners of property but his assessment of all special taxes so levied may be computed and made upon the valuation of property as fixed by the Board of Equalization for State and county purposes, and as appears upon the assessment roll in the same year.

SEC. 8.—*Special Tax Levy—A Lien Upon the Property—Assessor Must Keep Separate List and Get Separate Receipts.* Said special taxes so levied as aforesaid shall become a lien upon the property so assessed from the date of assessment, and shall be due and payable at the same time as State and county taxes. and in all respects are to be collected in the same way, except that the Assessor must keep a separate list or assessment roll thereof, and when paid must be named in his receipt to the taxpayer as a separate item, and he must pay them to the County Treasurer as he pays other taxes; but at the time of payment he must specify to the Treasurer what taxes they are, and take a separate receipt therefor and keep separate accounts thereof.

SEC. 9.—*Special Tax—Compensation of Assessor* The Assessor shall receive two per centum on all such special taxes so collected by him, having first rendered his account thereto. and the same being allowed by the Board of County Commissioners, and shall be paid out of said special tax.

SEC. 10.—*Special Tax—Provision for Blanks—Exemptions of Independent Districts.* The Board of County Commissioners shall furnish the Assessor with such blanks as are needed to comply with the provisions hereof. The provision of this act for the levy and collection of taxes shall not apply to independent districts now established, which have special laws for the collection of school taxes.

SEC. 11.—*Investment of Funds.* Whenever there shall have accumulated in the hands of the Treasurer of any school district in this State moneys belonging to said school district to an amount in excess of the amount which, in the opinion of the School District Board of said district, shall be necessary for the necessary current expenses of maintaining the schools in said district, the same shall be invested by said Board in United States bonds, State bonds, State warrants or county warrants. when the market value thereof is not below par. And said Board shall deposit said securities in some safe deposit, and they shall there be kept until it shall become necessary to convert the same into money for school district purposes, to be determined by said Board.

SEC. 12.—*New License Fund—Collection and Payment to*

Treasurer On the first Monday in each month the collector must return to the Auditor all licenses unsold and be credited therewith, and must, with the Auditor, appear at the Treasurer's office and pay into the county treasury all moneys collected for licenses sold during the preceding month, take the Treasurer's receipt therefor and file the duplicate thereof with the Auditor. The Auditor must credit the collector and charge the Treasurer therewith.

SEC. 13.—*Apportionment of the License Money.* Fifty per cent. of all moneys paid for licenses shall be applied to and constitute a part of the School Fund of the school district in which said licenses are collected, forty per cent. to the General Road Fund of the county in which said licenses are collected and ten per cent. shall be paid into the State treasury: *Provided.* That forty per cent. of all moneys paid for licenses by applicants within incorporated towns, cities, and villages, or cities acting under special charters shall be paid by the County Treasurer to the municipal authorities of such town, city, or village for general revenue purposes of such town, city, or village; fifty per cent. of said moneys so paid for licenses are to be applied and constitute a part of the School Fund of the school district in which said licenses are collected, and ten per cent. shall be paid into the State treasury.

SEC. 14.—*Collector's Report.* The Collector shall file with the Treasurer a statement or report each quarter showing the amount of licenses collected in each school district, incorporated town, city, or village, or city acting under special charter.

CHAPTER VIII.—TEACHERS AND TEACHERS' INSTITUTES.

SECTION 1.—*Registers and Reports.* Teachers of the public schools must be furnished with a school register by the Trustees of the district, for the purpose of registering the names of their pupils and their daily attendance at school, and at the close of the term said register must be delivered to the Clerk of the Board of Trustees of the district; and the teacher must also be furnished with a blank report by said Trustees, which report said teacher must fill up according to the heading of same and transmit it to the County Superintendent of the county at the close of the term; and no teacher shall be allowed an order in excess of ninety per cent. of his or her salary until said report is made out and transmitted.

SEC. 2.—*General Duties.* Every teacher in the public schools may suspend for good cause any pupil and report such suspension to the Board of Trustees for review. If the action of the teacher is sustained by the Board, the pupil may be censured and returned to the school or expelled from school as in the judgment of the Board seems proper, but if not sustained, the teacher may appeal to the County Superintendent, whose decision shall be final. Every teacher shall make reports, in addition to those mentioned elsewhere in said act, which may be required by the State

Superintendent. County Superintendent, or by the school district Board of Trustees; shall use the text books provided for the schools of the State; enforce the Course of Study and the rules and regulations prescribed by the State Superintendent; hold pupils to a strict account for disorderly conduct or improper language in and about the building, on the play grounds and on the way to and from school; shall keep himself or herself above reproach and endeavor to impress upon the minds of the pupils the principles of truth, justice, morality, patriotism and refinement and to avoid idleness, falsehood, profanity, vulgarity and intemperance; give attention during every school term to the cultivation of manners, and devote not less than thirty minutes each week to the systematic teaching of kindness of pupils to one another and toward domestic animals and other living creatures.

SEC. 3.—*Compensation.* No teacher shall be entitled to or receive any compensation for the time he or she teaches in any public school without a certificate valid or in force for such time in the county where such school is taught, except that if a teacher's certificate shall expire by its own limitation within six weeks of the close of a term such teacher may finish such term without reexamination or renewal of his or her certificate.

SEC. 4. *Prohibitions.* No books, papers, tracts or documents of a political, sectarian or denomination character must be used or introduced in any school established under the provisions of this act, and any and every political, sectarian or denominational doctrine is hereby expressly forbidden to be taught therein; nor shall any teacher or any district receive any of the public school moneys in which the schools have not been taught in accordance with the provisions of this act.

SEC. 5.—*School Year and School Month.* The school year within this State shall commence on the first Monday in September in each year. A school month is four weeks of five school days each.

SEC. 6.—*School Age Defined.* School age as herein used is defined as all persons between the age of five and twenty-one years.

SEC. 7.— *Institute Call Notice.* The County Superintendent of each county in this State must hold annually a teachers' institute at such time as he may designate, and such institute must continue in session not less than five nor more than fifteen days. He must give at least ten days' notice of the time and place of holding such institute by publication in some newspaper published in the county or by a written notice to each qualified teacher in the county. *Provided,* that two or more adjoining counties may unite in holding a joint institute under the joint supervision of the County Superintendents of such counties.

SEC. 8.— *Institutes—Teachers Shall Attend.* It is the duty of all teachers engaged in the county and of all persons holding certificates, to attend such institute and to participate in the exercise thereof, and all teachers who may have charge of schools at the time of holding the annual institute must adjourn their schools for the time during which the institute is held. *Provided,* that when joint institutes are held in accordance with the provisions of Section 51* it shall be the duty of all teachers in said counties and of all persons holding certificates therein, to attend such joint institute.

SEC. 9. *Institutes Adjournment of Schools.* All teachers who may adjourn school for the purpose of attending any annual county or joint institute must be allowed the same pay while in actual attendance as when teaching, and the County Superintendent must certify to the number of days attendance of each teacher, and the Trustees of the several districts must count them as so many days lawfully employed.

SEC. 10.— *Institutes — Assistants — Provisions for Expense.* The County Superintendent shall procure the services of one or more competent persons to assist in conducting said institute ; he must also provide a building, lights, stationery, janitor service, and all things necessary for the holding of the institute ; and must present an itemized account of such expenses not to exceed one hundred and fifty dollars, exclusive of the amount received from fees of applicants for teachers' certificates to the Auditor of his county, and the County Auditor shall issue a warrant in favor of the County Superintendent equal to the amount of such expenses. *Provided.* In case joint institutes are held as provided in Section 7, the County Superintendents of the counties holding such institutes shall each present an itemized account of such expenses as aforesaid to the Auditor of his county and the expenses thereof shall be borne equally by such counties, and the County Auditor shall issue a warrant in favor of the County Superintendent for the part chargeable against such county.

CHAPTER IX.—FREE TEXT BOOK LAW.

An Act to Provide for the Free and Uniform Text Books for the Public Schools of the State of Idaho.

Be it Enacted by the Legislature of the State of Idaho:

SECTION 1. The Governor of the State of Idaho is hereby authorized and empowered to appoint five persons, one of whom shall be the State Superintendent of Public Instruction, and four of whom shall be educators of the State of Idaho, who shall constitute a State Board of Text Book Commissioners, and who shall hold office until they have complied with the duties hereinafter imposed.

SEC 2. The said Board of Text Book Commissioners shall meet at the State Capitol, in the Senate chamber, on the first Monday in May, 1899, for the purpose of selecting and adopting a uniform series of text books for use in all the public schools of the State. Said Board shall have power to formulate rules for its own government and three members shall constitute a quorum.

*Section 7. Chapter 8.

SEC. 3. Immediately upon the approval of this Act, the State Superintendent of Public Instruction shall advertise for at least thirty days in two newspapers published in the State, giving notice that the Text Book Commissioners will meet as hereinbefore provided, and will consider all offers and proposals for supplying the State of Idaho with a uniform series of text books for use in all public schools of said State for a term of six years from and after the first day of September, 1899, in the following branches, to-wit: Spelling, Reading, Writing, Arithmetic, Geography, Grammar, Physiology and Hygiene, Civil Government, History of the United States, and in all other branches taught in the common, graded, and high schools of the State. Said proposals shall state the price at which said books will be furnished free on board the cars at the places designated by the said Commission. *Provided*, That the price paid for the books so adopted and used in the public schools shall not exceed the price at which said books shall be sold by said publishers to other purchasers during the existence of their contract with the State.

SEC. 4. It shall be the duty of the said Board of Text Book Commissioners to meet at the time and place mentioned in said notice, and to carefully consider all proposals made to them for the furnishing of the said text books as hereinbefore provided, and said Board shall select and adopt such text books for use in all the public schools, as will in their judgment best subserve the interests and promote the progress of the public schools in the State. The series of text books so selected and adopted by the said Board of Text Book Commissioners, shall be certified to by the Chairman, and said certificate with a copy of all books named therein, must be placed on file in the office of the State Superintendent of Public Instruction. Such certificate must contain a complete list of all books adopted by the said Board, giving the price for which each kind and grade of books will be furnished, and the name and address of the publisher agreeing to furnish the same. The said books named in the said certificate shall for a period of six years from and after the first day of September, 1899, be used in all the public schools of the State to the exclusion of all others.

SEC. 5. The said Board of Text Book Commissioners shall have power to make such contracts and agreements with publishers as they shall deem necessary for the best interests of the public schools of the State, and shall require of all publishers contracting and agreeing to furnish books adopted by said Commissioners to furnish bonds in double the amount in value of the books to be furnished, for the faithful performance of the conditions of said contract.

SEC. 6. Immediately after the filing of said certificate in his office, the State Superintendent of Public Instruction shall have prepared printed lists of the text books adopted by said Board, with the price of each of said books as certified to in said certificate and shall forward the same to the County Superintend-

ents of the several counties of the State, who shall immediately
forward one list to each Trustee and to each teacher in his county.

SEC. 7. It shall be the duty of all book publishers furnishing books to the State of Idaho under this Act to keep the books
they agree to furnish, on hand at all times at their places of
business.

SEC. 8. Not later than the first Monday in August, 1899,
and at such other times as may be necessary to properly supply
the schools of said district the Chairman of each of the several
Boards of Trustees of the county shall forward to the County
Superintendent of his county a list of the kind of books, and the
number of each kind, which will be required to supply the pupils of
the public schools of his district. Immediately upon the receipt of
this requisition from the Chairman of the Board of Trustees, the
County Superintendent shall order from the nearest book publisher or publishers furnishing said books designated therein, and
upon receipt of the duplicate bills from said publishers, and upon
comparison with the original bills sent to the Trustee or other
person to whom the order was consigned, and after comparing
the same with the published price furnished him by the State
Superintendent as hereinbefore provided, shall order the County
Treasurer to remit the purchased price to the said publishers from
the funds of said district: *Provided,* That if the district had no
funds to its credit in the hands of the County Treasurer, then the
said County Treasurer shall at once remit from the Current Expense Fund of the county, the same to be reimbursed to the
Current Expense Fund of the county, from the funds of the district as soon as the amount has been paid into the treasury to
the account of said district. And: *Provided, further,* That if
from any cause the accounts are not paid within ninety days, the
same shall draw interest at the rate of seven per cent. per annum
from the date of the shipment of the books to the date of payment.

SEC. 9. The County Superintendent and the County
Treasurer shall each keep an account of all books ordered, showing the number of the district, the number and kind of books, the
date of the order, the place from whence ordered, the date and
the amount of the remittance and such other items as will in
their judgement render the whole transaction easily understood.
Provided, That the Trustees of each district shall determine
whether or not the text books for said district shall be free text
books, and if it shall be determined by said Trustees that said
text books shall not be free then any parent or guardian or other
person having the legal or actual control of a child or children,
shall be required to purchase necessary books for such child or
children from the Trustees of his district at actual cost to t hat
district, and the Trustees shall pay the purchase price back into
the treasury, the same to be placed to the credit of said district:
Provided, That in cases where it is deemed by said Trustees that
any parent or guardian is unable to pay for said text books, the
same may be furnished free.

SEC. 10. The Clerk of the Board of Trustees is hereby

made the custodian of the text books belonging to the district.
and he shall, on the morning of the opening of the school or prior
thereto, count out the number of the books belonging to the district, noting carefully the condition of said books, and placing
the same in the hands of the teacher, taking a receipt for the
same and at the end of the term of the school the said Clerk of
the Board of Trustees shall receive the said books from the
teacher giving his receipt for them, and any missing or destroyed
books shall be accounted for by the teacher; *Provided*, That
the pupils shall be responsible through his parents or guardian,
to the district, if the responsibility is fixed upon said pupil, and:
Provided, further, That no one shall be responsible for the
natural wear and tear of the books. In the interim of the sessions
of the school, the Clerk of the Board of Trustees shall safely keep
the books, and use due diligence in their preservation.

SEC. 11. In connection with the text books that shall
have been adopted; the Board of Text Book Commissioners is
authorized to prepare such suggestions and outlines as in their
judgment will be useful to the teachers and schools of the State,
which said suggestions and outlines shall be printed and distributed to the teachers and Trustees of the State free of charge.
by the State Superintendent of Public Instruction. In addition
to the suggestions and outlines hereinabove mentioned, the State
Superintendent is authorized and it shall be her duty to prepare
and have printed such regulations as she may deem may be necessary, in regard to the care and custody of the books, and the
keeping of the accounts between the districts and the several
companies, and such regulations shall be binding on the County
Treasurer, County Superintendent, teachers and Trustees.

SEC. 12. The said Board of Text Book Commissioners
shall each receive the sum of six dollars per day and in addition
thereto each shall receive his actual and necessary expenses
while in the discharge of his official duties including the time actually and necessarily consumed in going to and returning from
the meeting of the commission.

SEC. 13. There is hereby appropriated the sum of one
thousand dollars or so much thereof as may be necessary, to
carry out the provisions of this act.

SEC. 14. All acts and parts of acts in conflict with this
act are hereby repealed.

SEC. 15. Whereas an emergency exists. this act shall take
effect and be in force from and after its passage.

Approved March 9, 1899.

CHAPTER X.—COMPULSORY EDUCATION.

SEC. 1. *Duties of Parents or Guardians - Proviso.* Every parent. guardian or other person in the State of Idaho having
control of a child or children between the ages of eight and fourteen years shall be required to send such child or children to a

public school for a period of twelve weeks in each school year, at
least eight weeks of which shall be consecutive, unless such child
or children are excused from such attendance by the Board of
School Trustees of the school district in which such parents or
guardians reside, upon it being shown to their satisfaction that
the bodily or mental condition of such children has been such
as to prevent his, her or their attendance at school, or application
at study for the period required, or that such child or children
are taught in a private school or at home in such branches as are
usually taught in a primary school, or have already acquired the
ordinary branches of learning taught in the public schools:
Provided, In case a public school shall not be taught for a period
of twelve weeks, during the year, within three miles by the nearest traveled road of the residence of any such parent or guardian
within the school district, he or she shall not be liable to the provisions of this act.

SEC. 2.—*Duties of Trustees* It shall be the duty of the
Board of School Trustees of each district in the State, on or before the first Monday in September in each year, to furnish the
principal in each public school taught in the district with a list
of all children in the school district between the ages of eight and
fourteen years, said list to be taken from the report of the School
Census Marshal.

SEC. 3.—*Duty of Teachers—Monthly Reports.* At the be-
ginning of each school month thereafter it shall be the duty of the
principal of each school in such district to report to the Board of
School Trustees of such district the names of all children attending school during the previous school month.

SEC. 4.—*Violation of the Law—How Proceedings are Begun
—Proviso.* When it shall appear, at the expiration of three
school months, to the Board of School Trustees that any parent,
guardian or other person having charge or control of any child
or children shall have failed to comply with the provisions of this
act, the Board shall cause demand to be made upon such parent,
guardian or other person for the amount of the penalty hereinafter provided, when, if such parent, guardian or other person
shall neglect or refuse to pay the same within five days after the
making of said demand, the Board shall commence proceedings
in the name of the school district for the recovery of the fine
hereinafter provided before any court having jurisdiction: *Provided,* That nothing in sub-division 1 shall apply to any child
or children who are actually and necessarily compelled to labor
for the support of a parent or parents.

SEC. 5.—*Penalty—Disposal of Fines Arising From Such
Funds.* Any parent, guardian or other person having control or
charge of any child or children, failing to comply with the provisions of this act, shall be liable to a fine of not less than five
dollars for the first offense, nor less than ten dollars, nor more
than fifty dollars for the second and each subsequent offense, be-
side the cost of collection. All fines collected under the provisions of this act shall be paid into the county treasury, the

same to be placed to the credit of the school district collecting the same.

SEC. 6.—*Trustees' Annual Notice.* The Board of School Trustees in each district shall cause to be posted annually in three public places in the district notices of the requirements and penalties of this law.

CHAPTER XI.—School Bonds.

SECTION 1.—*Election—Limit of Issue—Rate of Interest—Purpose.* The Board of School Trustees of any school district may, whenever a majority so decide, submit to the electors who are residents, freeholders or heads of families of the district, the question whether the Board be authorized to issue coupon bonds to a certain amount, not to exceed four per cent of the taxable property in said district, and bearing a certain rate of interest, not exceeding eight per centum per annum, and payable and redeemable at a certain time, for the purpose of building or providing a school house in said district with all necessary furniture, as desks, blackboards, globes, charts, outline maps, etc., and the Board of School Trustees of any school district, which has issued bonds for any of the purposes enumerated in this section, may submit to the electors of such district the question whether the Board shall be authorized to issue coupon bonds to refund or take up any of the bonded indebtedness of such district, at a rate of interest not exceeding eight per cent. per annum.

SEC. 2.—*Manner of Holding Election.* Such elections must be held in the manner prescribed for elections in this act. The ballots must contain the words "Bonds Yes" or "Bonds No." If two-thirds of the votes cast at such election are "Bonds Yes" the Board of Trustees must issue such bonds in such forms as the Board may direct; they must bear the signature of the Chairman of the Board of Trustees and be countersigned by the Clerk of the school district, and coupons attached to the bonds must be signed by said Chairman and said Clerk; and each bond so issued must be registered by the County Treasurer in a book provided for that purpose, which must show the number and amount of each bond and the person to whom the same is issued, and the said bonds must be sold by the said school Trustees as hereinafter provided.

SEC. 3.—*Notice of Sale.* The school Trustees must give notice in some newspaper published in the State, for a period of not less than four weeks to the effect that said school Trustees will sell said bonds, briefly describing the same, and stating the time when, and the place where said sale will take place: *Provided,* That the said bonds must not be sold for less than their par value, and the Trustees are authorized to reject any bids and to sell said bonds at private sale if they deem it for the best interest of the district, and all money arising from the sale of said bonds must be paid forthwith into the treasury of the county in which said district may be located, to the credit of said district, and the same are immediately available for any of the purposes authorized by this chapter.

SEC 4. The faith of each school district, is solemnly pledged for the payment of the interest and the redemption of the principal of all bonds, which are issued under this act. And for the purpose of enforcing the provisions of this act, each school district is a body corporate, and may sue and be sued by or in the name of the Board of School Trustees of said district.

SEC. 5.—*Interest—Loaning of Sinking Fund.* The school Trustees of each district must ascertain and levy annually the tax necessary to pay the interest as it becomes due and a Sinking Fund to redeem the bonds at their maturity, and said tax is a lien upon the property of said school district and must be collected in the same manner as other taxes for school purposes: *Provided,* That the said Sinking Fund may, at the discretion of the Board, be loaned on first mortgage or improved farm lands, but no loan shall exceed one-third of the market value of the land, exclusive of the improvements thereon, given as security for such loans. The annual interest on all loans herein provided for shall be seven per cent., or may be invested in United States bonds, State bonds, county or State warrants, when the market value thereof is not below par, at the discretion of said Board.

SEC. 6.—*Redemption.* When the sum in the Sinking Fund equals or exceeds the amount of any bond then due, the County Treasurer shall post in his office a notice that he will, within thirty days from the date of such notice, redeem the bonds then payable, giving the number thereof; and preference must be given to the oldest issue; and if at the expiration of the said thirty days the holder or holders of said bonds shall fail or neglect to present the same for payment, interest thereon must cease; but the Treasurer shall at all times thereafter be ready to redeem the same on presentation, and when any bonds are so purchased or redeemed the County Treasurer must cancel the same by writing across the face of each bond, in red ink, the word "redeemed," and the date of such redemption.

SEC. 7.—*County Treasurer Must Pay Interest.* The County Treasurer must pay out of any moneys belonging to a school district, the interest upon any bonds issued under this chapter by such school district when the same becomes due, upon the presentation at his office of the proper coupon, which must show the amount due and the number of the bond to which it belonged; and all coupons so paid must be reported to the school Trustees at the first meeting thereafter.

SEC. 8.—*Trustees Issue Bonds.* The school Trustees of any district must cause to be printed or lithographed at the lowest rate, suitable bonds, with the coupons attached, when the same becomes necessary, and pay therefor out of any moneys in the county treasury to the credit of the school district.

SEC. 9.—*Penalty for Refusing to Pay.* If any of the school Trustees fraudulently fail or refuse to pay into the county treasury

the money arising from the sale of any bonds provided for by
this act, they are guilty of a felony.

CHAPTER XII.—INDEPENDENT SCHOOL DISTRICTS.

FREE SCHOOLS—INDEPENDENT DISTRICT.

**An Act to Amend Section Seventy-eight of an Act Entitled, "An Act to Establish
and Maintain a System of Free Schools." Passed by the Second
Session of the Legislature of the State of Idaho.**

Be it Enacted by the Legislature of the State of Idaho:

SECTION 1.—*Free Schools—Independent Ditricts.* That
Section Seventy-eight [78] of an act of the legislature of the State
of Idaho entitled, "An Act to Establish and Maintain a System
of Free Schools," approved March 11, 1893, be amended so as
to read as follows: Sec. 78. Whenever any school district
within this State, as defined by the Board of County Commissioners, has within its limits taxable property to the amount of one
hundred and fifty thousand dollars or over, as shown by the last
assessment roll for the county, it may be organized into an independent school district upon a vote of one-fifth or over, of those
within the district who are qualified to vote at school elections,
petitioning the said Board for the establishing of such district as an
independent school district, and if a greater number of such qualified voters do not remonstrate against such establishment, the Board
must clearly, by its order of record, define the boundaries of such
district, if not already done, and within one month, order that the
question of so establishing such independent school district must
be submitted to a vote of all the electors of the district, who,
under the provisions of this act, are authorized to vote for the levy
of taxes and issue of bonds, and must make the necessary ar-
rangements for such election, giving at least twenty days' notice
thereof, and the time and place of holding the same. If a majority of those so voting, vote in favor of so organizing such
independent district, said Board must make its order of record
and declare such district established, and designate it as the
independent school district, [state name and number of district]
in . . . . County, Idaho.

SEC. 2.—*Corporate Powers.* The district so established is
constituted a body corporate and succeeds to the title of all
property, rights and privileges, and assumes and must discharge
and pay all debts, obligations and duties belonging to or devolving
upon the old district or districts of which it is so formed and
established, and by its corporate name it may:

FIRST. Make contracts, sue and be sued.

SECOND. Take, hold and convey such real and personal
property only as is needed for actual school purposes.

THIRD. To have a corporate seal.

FOURTH. To choose such officers as are herein provided
for.

SEC. 3.—*Officers—Trustees—Terms.* The officers of such
district consist of a Board of Trustees, composed of six qualified

electors, who are resident freeholders within the district. The first Board of Trustees must be appointed by the Board of County Commissioners immediately after the district is so established and hold their offices for terms as follows, to-wit: Two, until the next school election under the provision hereof; two for two, and two for four years after such election and until their successors are elected and qualified, and said Board so appointing must designate the term of each Trustee so appointed.

Sec. 4.—*Election—Time—Notice.* There must be an election for two members of the Board of Trustees to be held on the first Monday of September following the establishment of such district, and biennially thereafter an election must be held to elect two Trustees. The Clerk of the Board must give at least ten days' notice of the time and place of such election, by publication in a newspaper, or by three posted notices in the district.

Sec. 5.—*Qualified Electors—Judges' Decision on Tie Vote.* At all elections under this chapter voters must have the same qualifications prescribed by this title for school elections. At such elections any person offering to vote may be challenged and required to take all oaths required of voters at the general elections in this State; and on refusing to take such oaths must not be allowed to vote, and the Board of Trustees must appoint for all such elections two Judges and one Clerk. Voting must be by ballot, and if upon counting the ballots there is a tie and three qualified persons have the highest and an equal number of votes, the Board of Trustees must select two from the three, and when there is a failure to elect by reason of a tie vote the Board of Trustees must select.

Sec. 6.—*Vacancies.* If any Trustee dies, removes from the district, or ceases to have the qualifications for such office, or from any cause his office is vacant, or he neglects or refuses to act, or without excuse ceases to attend the meeting of the Board for four consecutive regular meetings thereof, his office thereby becomes vacant, and a majority of said Board of Trustees may appoint another qualified person to fill his unexpired term.

Sec. 7.—*Pecuniary Interest.* No Trustee must be interested in any contract let or made by or with the Board, or with any officer thereof, or in any supplies furnished to or for said district, or a surety for the performance of any contract with said Board or district, or the agent or partner of any contractor with said Board or district ; and no action can be maintained or recovery had against said Board or district upon any contract or obligation in which any Trustee is so interested, but the same is void.

Sec. 8.—*Official Oath of Trustees.* Each Trustee must before entering upon the duties of his office, take and subscribe the official oath, which must be filed with the County School Superintendent.

Sec. 9.—*Organization of Board of Trustees.* Immediately after the appointment of such Trustees by the Board of County Commissioners, as above provided, and after such biennial el-

ection, the Trustees, or a majority thereof, must meet at the
school house and organize as a Board, and from their number
must select a Chairman, a Clerk and a Treasurer, or they may
elect as Treasurer some competent or responsible person who is
not a Trustee.

SEC. 10.— *Compensation of Trustees.* No school officer
whatever must receive any pay or compensation for his time or
services or, in any way be allowed to make any pecuniary profit
or gain by reason of his office ; and any school officer or person
who has the custody in any way of any school funds must give
bonds, with at least two good sureties, in double the amount of
funds likely at any time to be in his custody.

SEC. 11.—*Regular Meetings—Quorum.* Regular meetings
of the Board of Trustees must be held on the second Monday of
each month, and special meetings may be called by the Chairman of the Board, or by any two Trustees, by personal notice of
the time and place of such meetings to each member of the Board,
or, if he cannot be found, by leaving such notice at his place of
residence with some person of suitable age and discretion. Four
Trustees constitute a quorum for the transaction of any business,
but a less number may adjourn any regular meeting from time
to time, until a quorum can be obtained ; but no meeting of the
Board, not provided for by the rules or by law, is legal unless all
the members thereof have been notified as provided for in this section.

SEC. 12.—*General Duties and Powers of Board of Trustees.*
The Board of Trustees of said district must have power to and it
is their duty:

FIRST.—To make such by-laws for their own government and
for the government of the schools of the district as they may
deem expedient, not inconsisient with the provisions of this chapter.

SECOND.—To employ or discharge teachers, mechanics and la-
borers, and to fix, allow and order paid their salaries and compensation, and to determine the rates of tuition for non-resident pupils.

THIRD.—To levy a special tax if necessary, which when added
to the moneys apportioned by the County Superintendent of
schools, will be sufficient to provide funds for the maintenance
of the schools for nine months in each year ; the special taxes
levied by said Board of Trustees for the payment of interest on
bonds and Sinking Fund, for payment of bonds at maturity, together with the levy for maintenance of schools, shall not exceed
ten mills on the dollar.

FOURTH.—To provide furniture, fixtures and apparatus, and
for everything needed in the school house or for the use of the
board.

FIFTH.—To rent, repair and insure school houses and property,
and preserve the same for the benefit of the school of the district.

SIXTH.—To build or remove school houses and buildings, and
to purchase or sell school lots.

SEVENTH.—To suspend or expel pupils from school who refuse to obey the rules thereof, and to exclude from school, children under six years of age.

EIGHTH.—To determine the number and qualifications of teachers who shall be employed and the length of time the school shall be kept, to fix the time for opening or closing of school, and for the dismissal of primary pupils before the regular time of closing schools.

NINTH.—To require pupils to be furnished with the proper and suitable books as a condition of membership in the schools.

TENTH.—To exclude from the schools and the school libraries of said district all books, tracts, papers and catechisms of a sectarian nature.

ELEVENTH.—To require teachers to conform to the law and the regulation of the Board.

TWELFTH.—To protect the morals and the health of the pupils while at school.

SEC. 13.—*General Provisions, Not Contradictory — Govern Independent Districts.* All the provisions of this act providing for a public school system wherein not contradictory to or inconsistent with the provisions of this chapter, and which may be made applicable to the objects thereof, are adopted as part of the law governing the establishment and management of independent school districts.

CHAPTER XIII.
ACT AUTHORIZING INDEPENDENT DISTRICTS TO ISSUE BONDS.

SEC. 1.—*Trustees May Issue — Purpose — Limit of Issue.* Board of Trustees of any independent school district organized under any general or special law, may issue negotiable coupon bonds of their district for the purpose of paying, redeeming or refunding the principal of any of the outstanding bonded indebtedness of their district, whenever the same can be done to the profit or advantage of their district, and without the district incurring any additional indebtedness or liability exceeding in any year the income or revenue provided for such year.

SEC. 2.—*Bonds—Description of.*—Said bonds must bear interest at not exceeding six per centum per annum, payable semi-annually, at the office of the Treasurer of the district, or at such banking house in the city of New York as may be designated by the Board of Trustees ; and the principal of said bonds, or any part thereof, may, at the option of the district, be paid at any time after ten years, and must be paid within twenty years, from the time they are issued, and in the order in which they are issued and numbered.

Semi-annual interest coupons, covering the interest to grow due, must be attached to each bond ; the bonds must be signed by the presiding officer of the Board and attested to by its Secretary and the seal of the district, if it have a seal, and the coupons must be signed and the bonds registered by the Treasurer of the Board.

SEC. 3. — *Bonds — value of — Application of Proceeds.* —
No bond shall be sold at less than its par value, and the proceeds
thereof must be devoted to the payment, redemption or refunding
of the outstanding bonded indebtedness of the district.

SEC. 4.— *Election to Issue Bonds for Building, Improving,* ·
Etc. The Board of Trustees of any such independent district
may, whenever two-thirds of the Board so decide, submit to the
qualified electors of the district, at an election to be held for that
purpose, and to be called and conducted as other school elections
in said district, the question whether the Board shall be authorized to issue the negotiable coupon bonds of the district in an
amount to be mentioned in the notice of election, for the purposes of providing and improving school houses and grounds and
furniture, apparatus, and fixtures for said district, or for any or
either of said purposes ; and if at such election two-thirds of the
qualified electors of said district voting at said election assent
thereto, the Board of Trustees may issue such bonds of the district to the amount and for the purpose designated in said notice;
which bonds shall be in all respects similar to, and shall be
be signed, negotiated, registered, bear interest, and be made payable as provided in the last preceding section ; and no bond shall
be sold for less than its par value ; and the proceeds thereof must
be devoted to the purposes mentioned in said notice.

SEC. 5.—*Special Tax for Interest — Sinking Fund and Re*
demption. The Board of Trustees of any such district that has
issued bonds under either of the last two preceding sections must
annually levy upon all the taxable property of the district, in
addition to other authorized taxes, a tax sufficient to pay the interest on all bonds so issued as it falls due, and also to constitute
a Sinking Fund for the payment of the principal thereof within
twenty years from the time the bonds are issued ; which taxes
shall be levied, assessed, collected and paid over as other taxes
are levied, assessed, collected and paid over, in the district, and
shall be devoted to the payment of the principal and interest of
said bonds only; and the accumulated Sinking Fund may be used
for the redemption of said bonds at any time after ten years from
the date of their issue. Approved March 6, A. D., 1891.

SEC. 6.   Whereas an emergeny exists, therefor, this act
shall take effect and be in force from and after its passage.

CHAPTER XIV.
An Act to Validate and Legalize State, County, School, Municipal or Other Bonds Issued Under Acts of the First, Second, Third, and Fourth Sessions of the Legislature of the State of Idaho.

Be it Enacted by the Legislature of the State of Idaho:

SECTION 1.   All bonds heretofore duly issued under, in
pursuance or by virtue of, and in accordance with, the provisions
of any Act of the first, second, third or fourth sessions of the
Legislature of the State of Idaho are hereby declared to be good,
valid and binding obligations, any question as to the manner of

the passage of any such Act or Acts notwithstanding; and their validity shall not be questioned in any court.

Sec. 2. Whereas an emergency exists therefor this Act shall take effect and be in force from and after its passage.

Approved March 6, 1899.

CHAPTER XV.

A Joint Resolution to Submit to the Electors of the State of Idaho for Rejection or Approval, an Amendment to Section Eleven of Article Nine, of the Constitution of the State of Idaho, Relating to Investing of Public School Fund.

Be it Resolved by the Legislatue of the State of Idaho:

SECTION 1. That Section Eleven of Article Nine of the Constitution of the State of Idaho be amended to read as follows: Section 11. The permanent educational funds other than funds arising from the disposition of University lands belonging to the State, shall be loaned on first mortgage on improved farm lands within the State; State, United States, or school district bonds, or State warrants, under such regulations as the Legislature may provide: *Provided*, That no loan shall be made of any amount of money exceeding one-third of the market value of the lands at the time of the loan, exclusive of the buildings.

SEC. 2. The question to be submitted to the electors of the State, at the next general election shall be in form as follows, to-wit: "Shall Section 11 of Article Nine of the Constitution of the State of Idaho be amended to enlarge the powers of the State Board of Land Commissioners, in loaning school money."

CHAPTER XVI.—EDUCATION OF DEAF, DUMB AND BLIND.

SECTION 1.—*Annual Appropriation.* There is hereby appropriated, annually, the sum of six thousand (6,000) dollars or so much thereof as may be necessary for the education of the deaf, dumb and blind of this State, under the direction of the State Board of Education, and the Treasurer shall pay the same on the warrant of the Auditor for that purpose.

SEC. 2.—*Contract for Tuition.* The said Board of Education shall enter into contract with some one of the adjacent States or Territories having an institution for the education of the deaf, dumb and blind of the State of Idaho upon the most economical terms possible.

SEC. 3.—*Duty of the Board of Education to Ascertain Pupils Eligible.* It shall be the duty of the Board of Education to ascertain the number of deaf, dumb and blind in the State of school age and of sound mind and body, whose parents are not able to provide for their education, and as soon as practicable thereafter take the necessary steps for their education as provided for in Section 2 of this act.

SEC. 4—*Payment of Tuition—Rate.* The State or Territory in which such institution for the education of the deaf, dumb and blind is located, as designated by the said Board of Education, shall be paid from the appropriation made in section 1, of this act, of the rate of not to exceed three hundred dollars a year for each scholar's instruction and board, including board during vacation, on the certificate of the State Board of Education to be furnished to the State Auditor.

SEC. 5.—*Examination of Applicants—Contingent Expenses.* The State Board of Education is authorized to provide for the careful examination of all applicants for admission to the institution designated, and to audit and certify to the State Auditor all accounts for the expenses of designating said institution and conducting examinations, and all contingent expenses attending the same, and the accounts thereof shall be paid from the appropriation for this purpose made in Section 1 of this act.

SEC. 6.—*Emergency Clause—In Approval.* This act shall take effect and be in force from and after its passage and approval, an emergency existing therefor.

Approved March 14, A. D., 1891.

CHAPTER XVII.

An Act to Provide for taking the Census of the Deaf and Blind Children of School Age and Defining who are Deaf and Blind.

Be it Enacted by the Legislature of the State of Idaho:

SECTION 1. It is hereby made the duty of the Census Marshal of each school district in the State of Idaho, when he shall enumerate the children of school age in his district, to carefully ascertain what children in that district are deaf or blind as defined in Section 2 of this Act, and he shall note the name, age, and sex of such child or children, also the names of parents or guardian or other person having the legal or actual charge of such child or children, and shall report the same to the County Superintendent of Public Instruction, and said County Superintendent of Public Instruction shall include these items in his annual report to the State Superintendent of Public Instruction.

SEC. 2. All children between the ages of six and twenty-four years, who are too deaf or too blind to be educated in our public schools shall be deemed deaf and blind for the purposes of this Act.

SEC. 3. Whereas an emergency exists, therefore, this Act shall be in force from and after its passage.

Approved March 13, 1899.

CHAPTER XVIII.—ACT TO ENCOURAGE ARBORCULTURE.

SECTION 1.—*Designation of Arbor Day.* The Friday following the first day of May in each year shall hereafter be known throughout this State as Arbor day.

SEC. 2.—*Schools Shall Observe the Day—Manner—Purpose.* It shall be the duty of the authorities of every public school in this State to assemble the scholars in their charge on that day in the school building or elsewhere, as they may deem proper, and to provide for and conduct, under the general supervision of the County Superintendents of Public Instruction, such exercises as shall tend to encourage the planting, protection and preservation of trees and shrubs, and an acquaintance with the best methods to be adopted to accomplish such results.

SEC. 3.—*Program of Exercises.* The State Superintendent of Public Instruction shall have power to prescribe from time to time in writing a course of exercises in instructions in the subject hereinbefore mentioned, which shall be adopted and observed by the school authorities on Arbor Day, and upon receipt of copies of such course, sufficient in number to supply all the schools under their supervision, the County Superintendent of Public Instruction aforesaid shall promptly provide each of the schools under his charge with a copy, and cause it to be adopted and observed.

SEC. 4.—*Emergency Clause.* This Act shall take effect and be in force from and after its passage and approval, an emergency existing therefor.

SEC. 5.—*Repealing Clause.* All Acts and parts of Acts inconsistent with this Act are hereby repealed.

CHAPTER XIX.

An Act to Prevent the Spread of Contagious Diseases.

Be it Enacted by the Legislature of the State of Idaho:

SECTION 1. The owner, or agent of the owner, of a house in which a person resides who has the small-pox, diphtheria, scarlet fever or any other contagious or infectious disease, dangerous to the public health, and the physician called to attend the person or persons so affected shall, within twenty-four hours after becoming cognizant of the fact, give notice thereof to the Clerk of the Board of Trustees of the school district in which said person so afflicted resides, and said person so afflicted shall be kept away and apart from all other persons except those whose presence may be necessary to the physical or spiritual wellbeing of such person or persons.

SEC. 2. The school Trustees of the various school districts in the State, shall not allow any pupil to attend the public schools while any member of the household to which such pupil belongs is sick of small-pox, diphtheria, scarlet fever or other contagious or infectious disease, dangerous to the public health, or during the period of two weeks after the death, recovery or removal of such sick person; and any pupil coming from such household shall be required to present, to the teacher of the school the pupil desires to attend, a certificate, from the attending physician, of the facts necessary to entitle him to admission in accordance with the above regulations.

SEC. 3. Whenever any text-book or books, belonging to any school district, shall be in any house during the time that pupils residing in such house are prevented from attending the public school in accordance with the provisions of this Act, such book or books shall not be returned to such public school until the same shall have been thoroughly disinfected under the direction of the attending physician, who shall certify the same to the teacher of said school, or to the Clerk of the Board of Trustees in case the school is not in session at such time.

SEC. 4. Any school Trustees or other person violating any of the provisions of this Act shall be deemed guilty of a misdemeanor.

SEC. 5. Whereas an emergency exists therefor, this Act shall be enforced from and after its passage.

Approved March 13, 1899.

CHAPTER XX.—UNIVERSITY OF IDAHO.

SECTION 1.—*Location* There is hereby established in this State at the town of Moscow, in the County of Latah, an institution of learning by the name and style of the "University of Idaho."

SEC. 2. The government of the University shall vest in a Board of Regents to consist of nine members chosen from the State at large, which board the Governor shall nominate, and with advice and consent of the Senate, appoint. The term of office of said Regents shall be six years from the first Monday in February in the year in which appointed. *Provided.* That the Regents appointed in the year 1899 shall hold their offices during the following periods: Three shall be appointed for a term of two years, three shall be appointed for a term of four years, and three shall be appointed for a term of six years. The Governor shall have power to fill vacancies in the Board by appointment, which appointment shall be valid until the last day of the regular session of the Legislature following such appointment.

SEC. 3.—*Board of Regents a Body Corporate—Organization —Duties of Officers.* The Board of Regents and their successors in office shall constitute a body corporate by the name of "The Regents of the University of Idaho," and shall possess all the powers necessary or convenient to accomplish the objects and perform the duties prescribed by law, and shall have the custody of the books, records, buildings and other property of said University. The Board shall elect a President, Secretary and Treasurer, who shall perform such duties as shall be prescribed by the by-laws of the Board. The Secretary shall keep a faithful record of all the transactions of the Board and of the Executive Committee thereof. The Treasurer shall perform all the duties of such office, subject to such regulations as the Board may adopt, and for the faithful discharge of all his duties shall execute a bond in such sum as the Board may direct.

SEC. 4.—*Elections and Annual Meetings Fixed by By-Laws—Quorum.* The time of the election of the President, Secretary and Treasurer of said Board, and the duration of their respective terms of office, and the times for holding the regular annual meeting and such other meetings as may be required, and the manner of notifying the same shall be determined by the by-laws of the Board. A majority of the Board shall constitute a quorum for the transaction of business, but a less number may adjourn from time to time.

SEC. 5.—*Board of Regents—General Duties.* The Board of Regents shall enact laws for the government of the University in all its branches, elect a President and the requisite number of professors, instructors, officers and employees, and fix the salaries and the term of office of each, and determine the moral and educational qualifications of applicants for admission to the various Courses of Instruction; but no instruction, either sectarian in religion or partisan in politics shall ever be allowed in any department of the University, and no sectarian or partisan test shall ever be allowed or exercised in the appointment of Regents or in the election of professors, teachers or other officers of the University, or in the admission of students thereto, or for any purpose whatever. The Board of Regents shall have power to remove the President, or any professor, instructor or officer of the University, when, in their judgment, the interests of the University require it. The Board may prescribe rules and regulations for the management of the libraries, cabinet, museum, laboratories and all other property of the University and of its several departments, and for the care and preservation thereof, with penalties and forfeitures, by way of damages, for their violation, which may be sued for and collected in the name of the Board before any court having jurisdiction of such action.

SEC. 6.—*Power to Expend Income.* The Board of Regents are authorized to expend such portion of the income of the University Fund hereinafter created as they may deem expedient for the erection of suitable buildings and the purchase of apparatus, a library, cabinets and additions thereto.

SEC. 7.—*Annual report of Regents* At the close of each fiscal year, the Regents, through their President, shall make a report in detail to the Governor, exhibiting the progress, conditions and wants of the University, the Course of Study, the number of professors and students, the amount of receipts and disbursements, together with the nature, costs and results of all important investigations and experiments, and such other information as they may deem important.

SEC. 8.—*Duties of the President.* The President of the University shall be President of the Faculty or of the several faculties as they may be hereafter established and the executive head of the instructional force in all its departments; as such, he shall have authority, subject to the Board of Regents, to give general direction to the instruction and scientific investigation of the University, and so long as the interests of the institution require it, he shall be charged with the duties of one of the professorships.

SEC. 9. — *G vernment of the University.* The immediate
government of the University shall be entrusted to the Faculty,
but the Regents shall have the power to regulate the Course of Instruction and prescribe the books or works to be used in the several courses, and also to confer such degrees and grant such diplomas as are usual in universities, or as they shall deem appropriate, and to confer upon the Faculty by by-laws the power to
suspend or expel students for misconduct or other cause prescribed by such by-laws.

SEC. 10.—*Object of the University.* The object of the University of Idaho shall be to provide the means of acquiring a
thorough knowledge of the various branches of learning connected with scientific, industrial and professional pursuits, and
to this end it shall consist of the following colleges or departments, to-wit:

FIRST. The college or department of arts.

SECOND. The college or department of letters.

THIRD. The professional or other colleges or departments as
may from time to time be added thereto or connected therewith.

SEC. 11.—*Courses of Instruction.* The college or department of arts shall embrace courses of instruction in mathemate-
cal, physical and natural sciences, with their application to the
industrial arts, such as agricultural, mechanics, engineering,
mining and metallurgy, manufacturers, architecture and com-
merce in such branches included in the college of letters as shall
be necessary to a proper fitness of the pupils in the scientific and
practical courses for their chosen pursuits ; and, as soon as the
income of the University will allow, in such order as the wants
of the public shall seem to require, the said course in the sciences
and their application to the practical arts shall be expanded into
distinct colleges of the University, each with its own faculty and
appropriate title. The college of letters shall be co-existent with
the college of arts, and shall embrace a liberal course of instruction in language, literature and physiology, together with such
courses or parts of courses in the college of arts as the Regents of
the University shall prescribe.

SEC. 12. — *Who May be Students.* The University shall
be open to female as well as male students, under such regulations and restrictions as the Board of Regents may deem proper.

SEC. 13. — *Tuition.* No student who shall have been a
resident of the State for one year next preceding his admission
shall be required to pay any fees for tuition in the University, except in a professional department and for the extra studies. The
Regents may prescribe rates of tuition for any pupil in a professional department, or who shall not have been a resident as
aforesaid, and for teaching extra studies.

SEC. 14.—*Board of Regents—Organization.* The Board of
Regents herein provided for shall be appointed immediately after
this act becomes a law ; and within ninety days after the appointment of said Regents the Board shall meet at Boise City and

elect a President, Secretary and Treasurer thereof, and shall at
said meeting adopt by-laws for the government of said Board and
the officers chosen by virtue of this act.

SEC. 15.—*Special Appropriations.—How Expended.* The
sum of Fifteen Thousand Dollars is hereby appropriated out of
any money in the state treasury of Idaho, not otherwise appropriated, and the State Auditor is hereby authorized to draw his
warrant on the State Treasurer for said amount, and the State
Treasurer is hereby directed and commanded to pay the same, as
hereinafter provided, which money shall be expended for the following purposes, to wit:

FIRST. The purchase of a site or grounds for said University, said location to consist of not less than ten nor more
than twenty acres of ground, and for the improvement of the
same, and for keeping the same in repair.

SECOND. To advertise for and obtain plans and specifica-
tions for a University building under such rules and regulations
as the Board may impose.

THIRD. For the payment of the necessary expense of said
Board, as hereinafter provided.

SEC. 16.—*Executive Committee.* The President and Secretary ex-officio, and one member of the Board to be appointed by
the President thereof, shall constitute an Executive Committee of
said Board, whose duties shall be prescribed by the by-laws of
the Board.

SEC. 17.—*Transfer of Appropriations.* Upon executing and
filing with the State Treasurer a good and sufficient bond, in
whatever sum the Board of Regents shall direct, provided said
bond shall have been first approved by the State Attorney General, the State Treasurer shall pay over to the Treasurer of the
Board the sum of fifteen thousand dollars, or so much thereof as
may be available; and in the event said sum is not paid in full
upon the execution and delivery of said bond as aforesaid, then
the remainder of said bond shall be transferred to the Treasurer
of said Board as speedily as the fund shall accumulate therefor.

SEC. 18.—*Expenditure of Funds.* The Treasurer of said
Board shall, out of any moneys in his hands belonging to said
Board, pay all orders drawn upon him by the President and
Secretary thereof, when accompanied by vouchers fully explaining
the character of the expenditure, and the books and account of
the Treasurer shall at all times be open to the inspection of the
Board. The Treasurer shall make an annual report to the President of the Board of all transactions connected with the duties
of his office.

SEC. 19.—*University Tax Levy.* There shall be levied and collected annually a State tax of three-quarters of a mill for each dollar
of the assessed valuation of taxable property of the State of Idaho,
which amount, when so levied and collected, shall be appropriated
to a University Building Fund. to remain in the treasury subject
to the order of the Board of Regents; but in no event shall

said Board appropriate the fund thus collected, or any portion thereof, to any purpose other than that for which said fund was provided: and, *Provided, further,* That said tax shall not be levied and collected for a longer period than four years from the date hereof.—[As amended by the act of 1891.]

SEC. 20.—*Regents—Compensation for Expenses.* The Regents shall receive the actual amount of their expense in traveling to and from and in attendance upon all meetings of the Board, or incurred in the performance of any duty in pursuance of any direction of the Board; accounts of such expenses shall be duly authenticated and audited by the Board and be paid on their order by the Treasurer out of any funds belonging to the University not otherwise appropriated; no Regent shall receive any pay, mileage or per diem except as above prescribed.

SEC. 21.—*Date of Passage and Approval.* This Act shall take effect and be in force from and after its passage.

Approved January 30, 1889.

An Act to Provide for the Issue of State Bonds for the Construction, Improvement and Furnishing of the Public Buildings of the State, and the Improvement of the Grounds Adjacent Thereto, and Creating a Sinking Fund and Providing for Its Investment.

Be it Enacted by the Legislature of the State of Idaho:

SECTION 1. That for the purpose of providing money for the finishing and furnishing the State University of Idaho, improving the Idaho State Penitentiary, building and furnishing a hospital and other improvements for the Soldiers' Home, and repairing and improving the Capitol building, a loan of Forty-nine Thousand ($49,000) dollars is hereby authorized to be negotiated by a Board, consisting of the Governor, Treasurer, Secretary of State and Attorney General of the State of Idaho, on the faith and credit of the State of Idaho. The Treasurer of the State is hereby authorized, empowered and directed immediately on the passage of this act to issue forty-nine (49) bonds of the State of Idaho, to be known as Idaho Improvement Bonds, in the sum of One Thousand ($1000) Dollars each, payable in twenty years from the date of their issuance, to bear interest at the rate of five (5) per cent. per annum, payable semi-annually on the first day of January and July of each year, at a bank in the city of New York to be selected by the State Treasurer ; *Provided,* that said bonds shall be redeemable at the option of the State of Idaho at any time after the expiration of ten years from their date of issuacne, and said bonds shall be plainly numbered from one (1) to forty-nine (49) consecutively. *Provided,* that the State Board of Land Commissioners is hereby authorized and directed to invest any and all moneys in the General School Fund of the State in the bonds authorized by this act, at their par value ; the remainder of the issue to be negotiated by sale to the highest responsible bidder.

SEC. 2 The State Treasurer is hereby authorized, empowered and directed to cause to be printed or lithographed suitable bonds in proper form, with coupons attached, for the purpose of this act. All such bonds shall be signed by the Secretary of State with his own proper name, affixing his official character, and shall be authenticated by the great seal of the State, and shall also be signed or endorsed by the Governor of the State with his own proper name, affixing his official character, and shall then be delivered by the Secretary of State to the Auditor, who shall make and keep a register of such bonds, showing the number and amount of each bond, and then deliver the said bonds to the State Treasurer, and charge the State Treasurer on the books of the Auditor's office with the full amount of such bonds.

SEC. 3. At the time of issuing of said bonds under the provisions of this Act, the State Treasurer shall sign them with his own proper name, affixing his official character, and shall in like manner sign the coupons thereunto attached, and such signing shall bind the State. The coupons for the payment of interest shall be attached to said bonds in such manner that they may be taken off, without injuring or mutilating the bonds, and shall be severally numbered from one (1) to forty-nine (49), inclusive, each bearing the corresponding number of the bond to which it is attached. The Treasurer shall keep a register of all the bonds issued by him, showing the date of issuance, and shall deliver said bonds, with coupons attached as aforesaid, to the purchaser or purchasers upon the receipt of the purchase money therefor; and the money received from the sale of said bonds shall be by said Treasurer placed in certain funds hereinafter named, as hereinafter provided, none of said bonds, however, shall be sold for less than their face or par value. The expense of printing or lithographing and procuring said bonds with coupons attached shall be paid out of the fund arising from the sale of the bonds, a proportionate amount being paid from each fund hereinafter provided.

SEC. 4. For the purpose of creating a fund to pay the interest coupons and the principal of said bonds, the State Treasurer is hereby empowered and directed, from and after the passage of this Act, to set apart one-half of all moneys that shall be received by him on account of licenses of every kind and description collected under the revenue laws of the State, and the same shall constitute a separate and distinct fund, to be known as the State Improvement Fund. And the State Treasurer shall pay the interest on said bonds, when due, out of said fund, taking the coupons as his vouchers therefor. And after the expiration of ten (10) years from the issuance of any of said bonds, whenever there shall be five thousand ($5000) dollars or more in said fund, provided for in this section, over and above the amount required for the payment of interest coupons due, or to become due within the next ensuing six months, the Treasurer shall use such surplus money in the redemption of said bonds according to the number and date of their issue, of which the Treasurer shall give notice by publication once in a week in some newspaper published in the county of Ada, and from the date of the last publication of such notice, the bonds proposed to be redeemed shall cease to draw interest; and if any such bonds shall not be presented within sixty days from the date of the last publication of such notice, the Treasurer shall apply the money for the redemption of bonds next in order of the number and date of their issue.

SEC. 5. If at any time there shall not be sufficient moneys in said State Improvement Fund to pay the interest coupons or the principal of such bonds when due, the State Treasurer shall pay the same out of the General Fund of the State, and shall replace the amount so paid out of the fund last named whenever moneys derived from licenses shall be received.

SEC. 6. At any time prior to the time when the bonds provided in Section one [1] of this act shall become subject to redemption, as provided by this act, the amount of money in the Sinking Fund provided for by Section four (4) of this act shall exceed the amount required for the payment of interest coupons of such bonds due, or to become due within the next ensuing twelve months, the State Treasurer shall use such surplus in payment of any warrant drawn upon him by the State Auditor, and presented for payment and not paid for want of money in the fund upon which they are drawn properly applicable thereto, and shall register and endorse such warrants, as provided by Section two hundred and thirty-eight (238) of the Revised Statutes, and place the same, so endorsed, to the credit of the Sinking Fund aforesaid; and such warrants shall bear interest and be payable in due course as other outstanding warrants, and, when paid, the interest and principal thereof shall belong to the Sinking Fund aforesaid, and shall be in like manner reinvested until said bonds become redeemable as aforesaid.

SEC. 7. When the money arising from the sale of said improvement bonds is received by the State Treasurer, he shall notify the State Auditor of the amount of money so received, and the State Auditor shall thereupon credit the Treasurer's account with the amount of bonds sold and proceed to apportion the money so received to the funds following which are hereby created, to-wit: Fourteen thousand ($14.000) dollars to the University Improvement Fund, and twenty-six thousand ($26,000) dollars to the Penitentiary Improvement Fund, and three thousand ($3,000) dollars to the Soldiers' Improvement Fund. and six thousand ($6,000) dollars to the Capitol Building Improvement Fund. Should such bonds be sold for more than their face or par value, the premium thereon shall be apportioned to the funds by this section created in proportional amounts.

SEC. 8. All moneys paid or to be paid into the funds above described [Section 7,] are hereby appropriated for the uses and purposes in this Act provided. Fourteen thousand [$14,000] dollars shall be paid out for expenses incurred in finishing and furnishing the State University of Idaho. Twenty-six thousand

($26,000) dollars shall be paid out for expenses incurred in improving the Idaho State Penitentiary, and three thousand ($3,000) dollars shall be paid out for expenses incurred in building and furnishing a hospital and improving the Soldiers' Home, and Six thousand ($6,000) dollars shall be paid for expenses incurred in repairs and improving the Capitol building.

SEC. 9. No contract or award or understanding for repairs or improvements for the different institutions mentioned in this Act shall be made or entered into by the various governing Boards of the institutions herein mentioned, unless the same shall have been submitted to and approved by the Chairman of the State Board of Examiners, and at least one of the other members of said Board of Examiners.

SEC. 10. Moneys in the University Improvement Fund, the Penitentiary Improvement Fund, the Soldiers' Home Improvement Fund, and the Capitol Building Improvement Fund, shall be drawn therefrom only upon warrants issued by the State Auditor upon certificates signed by the Secretary and President, or Secretary and Chairman, of the several Boards of Regents, or Commissioners, or Trustees, of the different institutions, duly approved by the State Board of Examiners.

SEC. 11. This Act shall take effect and be in force from and after its passage, an emergency existing therefor.

Approved, March 9, 1899.

CHAPTER XXI.—LEWISTON STATE NORMAL SCHOOL.

SECTION. 1.—Location—Purpose of School—Proviso. That a Normal School for the State of Idaho is hereby established in the city of Lewiston, in the County of Nez Perce, to be called the "Lewiston State Normal School," the purpose of which shall be for training and educating teachers in the art of instruction and governing in the public schools of this State, and of teaching the various branches that pertain to a good common school education: Provided, That the Mayor and city council of the said city of Lewiston shall prior to the first day of May, eighteen hundred and ninety-three, donate to the Board of Trustees hereinafter named, as a site for the use of the said Lewiston State Normal School, ten acres of land, within the limits of the said city of Lewiston, known and described as a part of the City Park of Lewiston, and shall convey the same by a good and perfect title in fee simple to said Board of Trustees, who are hereby authorized and empowered to receive and hold the same, and the title thereto, in trust and for the use of the Lewiston State Normal School. And the Mayor and city council of the said city of Lewiston are hereby authorized and empowered to convey said site of ten acres to the said Board of Trustees as aforesaid.

SEC. 2. The said Lewiston State Normal School shall be under the direction of a Board of Trustees to be known as "The Board of Trustees of the Lewiston State Normal School." The said Board of Trustees shall consist of six members, to-wit: B.

F. Morris and C. W. Shaff, who shall hold their terms of office until January 27, A. D., 1901; Jno. P. Vollmer and Geo. E. Erb, who shall hold their terms of office until January 27, A. D., 1903; and James W. Reid and James W. Poe, who shall hold their terms of office until January 27 A. D., 1905, and their successors shall be appointed for the term of six years by the Governor of the State of Idaho, by and with the advice and consent of the Senate. Before entering upon the duties of his office, each of said Trustees shall take and subscribe an oath or affirmation before some person duly authorized to administer the same. that he will support the constitution of the United States and the State of Idaho, and will faithfully and impartially discharge the duties of the office of Trustee of the Lewiston State Normal School, which oath or affirmation shall be filed in the office of the Secretary of State.

SEC. 3.—*Organization—Quorum—Etc.* The said Board of Trustees may conduct its proceedings in such manner as will best conduce to the proper dispatch of business. A majority of the Board of Trustees shall constitute a quorum for the transaction of business but a less number may adjourn from time to time. No member of said Board of Trustees shall participate in any proceedings in which he has any pecuniary interest. Every vote and official act of the said Board of Trustees shall be entered on record. Said Board of Trustees shall have an official seal, which shall be judicially noticed. Said Board of Trustees may sue and be sued. No vacancy in the Board of Trustees shall impare the right of the remaining Trustees to exercise all the powers of the said Board of Trustees. At their first meeting, and annually thereafter, the said Board of Trustees shall elect from their number a President and a secretary. The State Treasurer shall be ex-officio Treasurer of the said Board of Trustees. It shall be the duty of the Secretary to keep an exact and detailed account of the doings of said Board, and itemized account of all expenditures authorized by said Board.

SEC. 4.—*General Powers and Duties of Trustees.* The said Board of Trustees are hereby authorized, and it is made their duty, to take and at all times to have general supervision and control of all buildings and property appertaining to said Normal School, and to have general charge and control of the construction of all buildings to be built. They shall have power to let contracts for buildings and completion of any such buildings, and the entire supervision of their construction.

SEC. 5.—*Funds—How Expended—Proviso.* One half of all funds appropriated for the use and benefit of Normal Schools in the State of Idaho, for the establishment and maintenance of State Normal Schools, shall be under the direction and control of said Board of Trustees subject to the provisions herein contained. The Treasurer of the Board shall pay out of such funds all orders or drafts for money to be expended under the provisions of this Act. Such orders or drafts to be drawn by the State Auditor on certificates of the Secretary countersigned by the President of the said Board of Trustees. No such certificates shall be given except upon accounts audited and allowed by said Board: *Provided.* The Board of Trustees of said Lewiston State Normal School may use all the funds in the State treasury arising from the sale of any part of said lands, until such time as another State Normal School shall be established: and, *Provided, further,* Not more than fifty thousand(50,000) acres of said lands shall ever be sold for said pupose of establishing and maintaining the Lewiston State Normal School, and said Board of Trustees shall never use more of said funds than necessary for the purpose of carrying out the provisions of this act.

SEC. 6.—*Regular Meetings.* The Board of Trustees shall hold two regular meetings annually at the said city of Lewiston, but special meetings may be called by the President of the Board by sending written notice at least ten days before such meeting to each member.

SEC. 7.—*Election of Teachers—Salaries—Removals.* The Board of Trustees shall have power to elect a principal and other teachers that may be deemed necessary, to fix the salaries of the same and to prescribe their duties. They shall have power to remove either the principal, assistant or teachers and appoint others in their stead.

SEC. 8.—*Course of Study.* It shall be the duty of the Board of Trustees to prescribe the Course of Study, and the time and standard of graduation, and to issue such certificates and diplomas as may from time to time be deemed suitable. These certificates and diplomas shall entitle the holder to teach in the public schools of any county in the State for the time and in the grade specified in the certificate or diploma.

SEC. 9.—*Text Books, Apparatus and Furniture.* The Board of Trustees shall prescribe the text books, apparatus and furniture, and provide the same together with all necessary stationery for the use of the pupils.

SEC. 10.—*Training or Model Schools.* The Board of Trustees shall, when deemed expedient, establish and maintain a training or model school or schools; in which the pupils of the Normal School shall be required to instruct classes under the supervision and direction of experienced teachers.

SEC. 11.—*Rules and Regulations.* The Board of Trustees shall ordain such rules and regulations for the admission of pupils to said Normal School as they shall deem necessary and proper. All classes may be admitted into the said Normal School who are admitted without restriction into the public schools of the State. *Provided.* The applicant, if a male, must be not less than sixteen years of age, or if a female, not less than fifteen years of age. Applicants must also present letters of recommendation from the County Superintendent of Public Instruction of the county in which they reside, certifying to their good moral character, and their fitness to enter the Normal School. Before entering all applicants must sign the following declaration: "We hereby declare that our purpose in entering the Lewiston

State Normal School is to fit ourselves for the profession of teach-ing, and that it is our intention to engage in teaching in the pub-lic schools of this State."

SEC. 12.—*Non-Resident Pupils.* Pupils from other States and territories may be admitted to all the privileges of the said Normal School, on presenting letters of recommendation from the Executive or State School Superintendent thereof, and the pay-ment of one hundred dollars. Pupils from other states shall not be required to sign the declaration named in the foregoing section.

SEC. 13.—*Lectures in Sciences and Arts.* Lectures in chem-istry, comparative anatomy, agricultural chemistry, and any other science or any other branch of literature that the Board of Trustees may direct, may be delivered to those attending such school in such manner and on such conditions as the Board of Trustees may prescribe.

SEC. 14.— *Traveling and Necessary Expenses of Trustees.* The actual and necessary personal expenses incurred by the mem-bers of said Board of Trustees, in carrying out the provisions of this act, shall be paid on the proper certificate out of any funds belonging to said Normal School in the hands of the Treasurer.

SEC. 15.—*Vacancies on Board of Trustees* It shall be the duty of the Governor of the State to fill by appointment all vacan-cies that may, from any cause, occur in the said Board of Trustees.

SEC. 16.—*Annual Report.* The President and Secretary of the Board of Trustees shall on the first day of January of each year, transmit to the Governor of the State, a full report of the doings of the said Board of Trustees, the progress and condition of said Normal School, together with a full report of the expend-itures of the same for the previous year, setting forth each item in full, and the date thereof and such recommendations as they deem proper for the good of said Normal School.

SEC. 17.—*School Discipline.* The Board of Trustees in their regulations. and the Principal and assistants in their supervision and government of said school, shall exercise a watchful guard-ianship over the morals of the pupils at all times during their at-tendance upon the same, but no religious or sectarian tests shall be applied in the selection of teachers, and none shall be adopted in said school.

Approved, Feb. 7, 1899.

CHAPTER XII.—LEWISTON STATE NORMAL SCHOOL.

An Act Providing for the Issue of State Bonds for the Purchase of Chemicals and Chemical and Physical Apparatus, and for the Erection of two Dormitories for the Lewiston State Normal School, and Prescribing how the Proceeds of the Sale of such Bonds shall be Expended.

Be it Enacted by the Legislatue of the State of Idaho:

SECTION. 1. That for the purpose of providing money for chemicals and chemical and physical apparatus, and for the erection of two dormitories for the Lewiston State Normal School,

located at Lewiston, in Nez Perce County, State of Idaho, a loan
of Seven Thousand Five Hundred (7,500) Dollars is hereby authorized to be negotiated by a Board consisting of Governor,
Treasurer, Secretary of State and Attorney General, of the State
of Idaho on the faith and credit of the State of Idaho, and
secured by the proceeds of the sale of State Normal School lands
and the timber thereon as hereinafter provided.

SEC. 2. The Treasurer of the State is hereby authorized,
empowered and directed immediately upon the passage of this
Act, to issue fifteen (15) bonds of the State of Idaho, to be known
as Idaho Lewiston State Normal School Bonds, in the sum of
Five Hundred (500) Dollars each, payable in twenty (20) years
from the date of their issuance, to bear interest at the rate of five
per cent. per annum, payable semi-annually on the first days of
January and July of each year at a bank in the city of New York
to be selected by the State Treasurer; said bonds however to be
redeemable at the option of the State of Idaho, at any time at the
expiration of ten (10) years from the date of their issuance, and
said bonds shall, be plainly numbered from one to fifteen (15)
consecutively.

SEC. 3. The State Treasurer is hereby further authorized,
empowered and directed, to cause to be printed or lithographed,
suitable bonds, in proper form, with coupons attached, for the
purposes of this Act. All such bonds shall be signed by the Secretary of State with his own proper name, affixing his official
character, and shall be authenticated by the Great Seal of the
State, and shall also be signed or endorsed by the Governor of the
State with his own proper name, affixing his official character,
and shall then be delivered by the Secretary of State to the State
Auditor, who shall make and keep a register of such bonds, showing the number and amount of each bond, and then deliver the
said bonds to the State Treasurer, and charge the State Treasurer
on the books of the Auditor's office with the full amount of each
bond.

SEC. 4. At the time of issuing said bonds under the provisions of this Act, the State Treasurer shall sign them with his
own proper name, affixing his official character, and shall in like
manner sign the coupons thereunto attached, and such signing
shall bind the State. The coupons for the payment of interest
shall be attached to said bonds in such manner that they may
be taken off without injury or mutilating the bonds, and shall be
severally numbered from one to forty, inclusive, each bearing the
corresponding number of the bond to which it is attached. The
Treasurer shall keep a register of all the bonds issued by him
showing the date of issuance, and shall deliver said bonds with
the coupons attached as aforesaid, to the purchaser or purchasers,
upon the receipt of the purchase money therefor; and the money
received from the sale of said bonds shall be by said Treasurer
placed in a certain fund to be known as the Lewiston Normal
School Fund for chemical and physical apparatus and the erection of domitories, none of said bonds however shall be sold for

less than their face or par value. The expense of printing or
lithographing and procuring said bonds with coupons attached,
shall be paid out of the funds arising from the sale of said bonds.

SEC. 5. For the purpose of securing the payment of the
principal of the bonds provided for in this Act, the proceeds of
the sale of all the lands, or of timber growing thereon, granted
to the State of Idaho by the United States for State Normal
Schools are hereby set apart as a separate and distinct fund to be
known as the Normal School Sinking Fund; and after the payment of the principal and interest of the bonds provided for by
an Act providing for the issue of said bonds for the benefit of the
Albion State Normal School and the Lewiston State Normal
Schools, and prescribing how the proceeds of the sale of said
bonds shall be expended, ratified the seventh day of March, 1895;
and after the payment of the said principal of the said
bonds provided by this Act, then the proceeds of the sales
of said land or timber shall be paid into the General Fund
in the State treasury,until an amount, equal to the total amount
of interest that has theretofore been paid out of said General Fund
on said bonds, issued by the said two Acts hereinbefore named,
less the amount of interest that may have been paid into said
General Fund from investment of Normal School Sinking Fund
moneys in State warrants, as hereinafter provided for, has been
so paid into said General Fund. When the principal of said
bonds shall have been fully paid and the General Fund of the
State reimbursed for interest on said bonds provided in said two
Acts as herein specified, then and thereafter the proceeds of the
sales of such lands and timber shall be disposed of, as may by
law be provided.

SEC. 6. At any time after ten (10) years from the issuance
of said bonds, whenever there shall be ten thousand (10,000)
dollars of said Sinking Fund, the Treasurer of the State shall
make a "call" by publication for sixty (60) days in some daily
newspaper in this State, notifying all the parties interested that
certain bonds of said Normal School Bonds provided by the said
two Acts hereinbefore referred to, giving their numbers, will at a
certain date be paid at the office of said Treasurer, and the bonds
so called shall cease to bear interest from and after the date in
said "call" specified.

SEC. 7. At any time when money to the amount of One
Thousand Dollars or more is in said Sinking Fund it is hereby
made the duty of the State Treasurer to invest such money in
registered State warrants of this State, and in registered State
warrants only, and to hold such warrants until they are redeemed as a part of said Sinking Fund, and whenever State warrants so held by the Treasurer are paid, the Treasurer shall certify
the amount of interest that may have accrued thereon to the
State Auditor and the amount of such interest shall thereupon be
placed to the credit of and become a part of the General Fund of
the State, and the amount of the principal of said Sinking Fund
invested in such warrants shall upon the redemption of said war-

rants be returned to said Sinking Fund, to be reinvested in the same manner: *Provided*, That when the principal of said Sinking Fund is required for the redemption of the bonds called as provided for in this Act, such principal shall not be so invested in such warrants.

Sec. 8. For the prompt payment of the interest that may accrue upon said bonds there is hereby appropriated for each year out of any moneys in the State treasury not otherwise appropriated, an amount equal to the amount of said interest on said bonds as the same may become due, and for the payment of such interest when due the Treasurer of the State shall reserve any and sufficient of the funds in his hands, in preference to all other claims whatsoever, except the interest on bonds of the State heretofore issued pursuant to law.

Sec. 9. When the moneys arising from the sale of said bonds are received by the State Treasurer he shall notify the State Auditor of the amount of money so received, and the State Auditor shall thereupon credit the Treasurer's account with the amount of bonds sold.

Sec. 10. All moneys paid or to be paid into said the Lewiston State Normal School Fund, are hereby appropriated to the Lewiston State Normal School for the purposes of said two acts as hereinbefore stated and provided.

Sec. 11. The moneys in said Lewiston State Normal School Fund received from sale of bonds issued under this Act, and hereinbefore stated and provided, shall be paid out for the purchase of chemicals and chemical and physical apparatus, and for the erection and furnishing of the two dormitories for the Lewiston State Normal School.

Sec. 12. The moneys in the said Lewiston State Normal School Fund, as hereinbefore provided in this Act, shall be drawn therefrom only upon warrants issued by the State Auditor upon certificates of the Secretary of the Board of Trustees of said Lewiston Normal School, countersigned by the President thereof, as provided in Section five [5] of "An Act to establish a State Normal School at Lewiston," etc.: Approved February 7, 1899, and approved by the State Board of Examiners.

Sec. 13. Whereas an emergency exists therefor this Act shall be in force and effect from and after its passage and approval.

Became a law without Executive Approval March 9, 1899.

CHAPTER XXIII.—Albion State Normal School.

Section 1.—*Location—Purpose—Proviso.* That a Normal School for the State of Idaho is hereby established at or near the town of Albion, in the County of Cassia, to be called the "Albion State Normal School," the purpose of which will be for training and educating teachers in the art of instruction and governing in the public schools of this State, and of teaching the various branches that pertain to a good common school education: *Pro*

rided. That J. E. Miller, of the said town of Albion, shall prior
to the first day of May, eighteen hundred and ninety-three, donate to the Board of Trustees hereinafter named, as a site for the
use of the said Albion State Normal School, five acres of Lot 3,
Section 6, Township 12, S., R. 25 E., together with a permanent.
water right therefor and shall convey the same by a good' and
perfect title in fee simple to said Board of Trustees, who are
hereby authorized and empowered to receive and hold the same,
and the title thereto, in trust and for the use of the said Albion
State Normal School.

SEC. 2. That a non-partisan Board of Trustees to be
known as "The Board of Trustees of the Albion State Normal
School" consisting of five members, no more than three of whom
shall be of the same political party, is hereby created for the
management and control of the Albion State Normal School.
Said Trustees shall be appointed by the Governor by and with
the advice and consent of the Senate, for a term of two years and
until their successors are appointed and qualified, and before entering upon the duties of their office each of said Trustees shall
take and subscribe an oath or affirmation that he will support
the constitution of the United States and the constitution and
laws of the State of Idaho, and will faithfully and impartially
discharge the duties of said office, which oath or affirmation shall
be filed in office of Secretary of State.

SEC. 3. All the rights, powers, duties and titles to real estate or personal property belonging to or vested in said Albion
State Normal School, are hereby vested in the Trustees of said
school herein provided for.

SEC. 4.—*Organization—Quorum—Etc.* The said Board of
Trustees may conduct its proceedings in such manner as will best
conduce to the proper dispatch of business. A majority of the
Board of Trustees shall constitute a quorum for the transaction
of business, but a less number may adjourn from time to time.
No member of said Board of Trustees shall participate in any
proceedings in which he has any pecuniary interest. Every vote
and official act of the said Board of Trustees shall be entered on
record. Said Board of Trustees shall have an official seal, which
shall be judicially noticed. Said Board of Trustees may sue and
be sued. No vacancy in the Board of Trustees shall impair the
right of the remaining Trustees to exercise all the powers of the
said Board of Trustees. At their first meeting, and annually
thereafter, the said Board of Trustees shall elect from their number a President and a Secretary. The State Treasurer shall be ex-
officio Treasurer of the said Board of Trustees. It shall be the
duty of the Secretary to keep an exact and detailed account of
the doings of said Board, and an itemized account of all expend-
itures authorized by said Board.

SEC. 5.—*General Powers and Duties of Trustees.* The said
Board of Trustees are hereby authorized, and it is made their
duty, to take and at all times to have general supervision and
control of all buildings and' property appertaining to said Normal

School, and to have general charge and control of the construction of all buildings to be built. They shall have power to let contracts for buildings and completion of any such buildings, and the entire supervision of their construction.

SEC. 6.—*Funds—How Expended—Proviso.* All funds appropriated for the use and benefit of said Normal School, ·from every source, including the pro rata share of the available proceeds of sales of land, granted by the government of the United States to the State of Idaho, for the establishment and maintenance of the State Normal Schools, due to said Normal School, shall be under the direction and control of said Board of Trustees subject to the provision herein contained. The Treasurer of the Board of Trustees shall pay out of such funds all orders or drafts for money to be expended under the provisions of this Act. Such orders or drafts shall be drawn by the State Auditor on certificates of the Secretary countersigned by the President of said Board of Trustees and approved by the State Board of Examiners. No such certificates shall be given except on accounts audited and allowed by said Board of Trustees.

SEC. 7.—*Regular Meetings.* The Board of Trustees shall hold two regular meetings annually, at the said town of Albion, but special meetings may be called by the President of the Board by sending written notice at least ten days before such meeting to each member.

SEC. 8.—*Election of Teachers—Salaries—Removals.* The Board of Trustees shall have power to elect a principal and all other teachers that may be deemed necessary, to fix the salaries of the same and to prescribe their duties. They shall have power to remove either the Principal, assistant or teachers and appoint others in their stead.

SEC. 9.—*Course of Study—Value of Certificates.* It shall be the duty of the Board of Trustees to prescribe the course of study, and the time and standard of graduation, and to issue such certificates and diplomas as may from time to time be deemed suitable. These certificates and diplomas shall entitle the holders to teach in the public schools in any county in this State for the time and in the grade specified in the certificate or diploma.

SEC. 10.—*Text Books, Apparatus and Furniture.* The Board of Trustees shall prescribe the text books, apparatus and furniture, and provide the same together with all the necessary stationery for the use of the pupils.

SEC. 11.—*Training or Model Schools.* The Board of Trustees, shall, when deemed expedient, establish and maintain a training or model school or schools; in which the pupils of the Normal School shall be required to instruct classes under the supervision and direction of experienced teachers.

SEC. 12.—*Rules and Regulations.* The Board of Trustees shall ordain such rules and regulations for the admission of pupils to said Normal School as they shall deem necessary and proper. All classes may be admitted into the said Normal School who are admitted without restriction into the public schools of the State: *Provided*, The applicant, if a male, must be not less than sixteen years of age, or if a female not less than fifteen years of age. Applicants must also present letters of recommendation from the County Superintendent of Public Instruction of the county in which they reside, certifying to their good moral character, and their fitness to enter the Normal School. Before entering all applicants must sign the following declaration: "We hereby declare that our purpose in entering the Albion State Normal School is to fit ourselves for the profession of teaching, and that it is our intention to engage in teaching in the public schools of this State."

SEC. 13.—*Non-Resident Pupils.* Pupils from other States and Territories may be admitted to all the privileges of the said Normal School, on presenting letters of recommendation from the Executive or State School Superintendent thereof, and paying such tuition fee as the Board of Trustees may prescribe. Each of such pupils must sign the following declaration: "I hereby declare that my purpose in entering the Albion State Normal School is to fit myself for the profession of teaching."

SEC. 14.—*Lectures in Sciences and Arts.* Lectures in chemistry, comparative anatomy, mechanical arts, agricultural chemistry, and any other science or any other branch of literature that the Board of Trustees may direct, may be delivered to those attending such school in such manner and on such conditions as the Board of Trustees may prescribe.

SEC. 15.— *Traveling and Necessary Expenses of Trustees.* The actual and necessary personal expenses incurred by the members of said Board of Trustees, in carrying out the provisions of this act, shall be paid on the proper certificate out of any funds belonging to said Normal School in the hands of the Treasurer.

SEC. 16.—*Vacancies on Board of Trustees.* It shall be the duty of the Governor of the State to fill by appointment all vacancies that may, from any cause, occur in the said Board of Trustees.

SEC. 17.—*Annual Report.* The President and Secretary of the Board of Trustees shall on the first days of January and July of each year, transmit to the Governor of the State, a full report of the doings of the said Board of Trustees, the progress and condition of said Normal School, together with a full report of the expenditures of the same for the previous six months, setting forth each item of in full, and the date thereof and such recommendations as they deem proper for the good of said Normal School.

SEC. 18.—*School Discipline.* The Board of Trustees in their regulations, and the Principal and assistant in their supervision and government of said school, shall exercise a watchful guardianship over the morals of the pupils at all times during their attendance upon the same, but no religious or sectarian tests shall be applied in the selection of teachers, and none shall be adopted in the said school.

SEC. 19. Whereas an emergency exists therefor this Act shall take effect and be in force from and after its passage.

Approved, February 14, 1899.

INDEX.

GENERAL SCHOOL LAWS

OF THE STATE OF IDAHO.

GENERAL SCHOOL LAWS

GENERAL SCHOOL LAWS